Brad Richards

A HOCKEY STORY

PAUL HOLLINGSWORTH

NIMBUS
PUBLISHING

Nimbus Publishing Limited
PO Box 9166
Halifax, NS   B3K 5M8
(902) 455-4286

Printed and bound in Canada

Design: Troy Cole – Envision Graphic Design
Author photo: Steve Townsend/CTV Atlantic

Library and Archives Canada Cataloguing in Publication

Hollingsworth, Paul, 1969-
Brad Richards : a hockey story / Paul Hollingsworth.
ISBN 978-1-55109-633-9

1. Richards, Brad, 1980- 2. Hockey players—Canada—Biography. I. Title.

GV848.5.R53H64 2007   796.962092
C2007-904584-7

We acknowledge the financial support of the Government of Canada through the Book Publishing Industry Development Program (BPIDP) and the Canada Council, and of the Province of Nova Scotia through the Department of Tourism, Culture and Heritage for our publishing activities.

DEDICATION

For Dawson and Jamieson,
the bright lights in my life.

PHOTO CREDITS:

All numbers refer to page numbers in the text.

Athol Murray College of Notre Dame Archives: 5, 7, 9, 10

Scott Audette: 51, 54

Craig Campbell/Hockey Hall of Fame: 57

Steve Deschênes/Hockey Hall of Fame: 25

Andy Devlin/Hockey Hall of Fame: 67

Matthew Manor/Hockey Hall of Fame: 43, 49, 63, 66

Walt Neubrand/Hockey Hall of Fame: 58

The Richards family: 1, 3, 4(top), 4(bottom), 6, 8, 11, 13, 14, 16, 28, 29, 56, 59, 61(top), 61(bottom), 68, 69, 70, 71

Dave Sandford/Hockey Hall of Fame: 19, 20, 23, 26, 27, 33, 35, 37, 39, 45, 47, 53, 55, 60

Table of Contents

Foreword

WHEN PAUL HOLLINGSWORTH ASKED ME IF I WOULD BE INTERESTED IN WRITING THE FOREWORD TO THIS BOOK, I IMMEDIATELY SAID YES.

And then I had to laugh. Mostly at myself.

It is time for true confessions. The secret cannot be kept any longer. It must be said: I never thought Brad Richards would be a big-time NHL player. Heck, I wasn't so sure he would ever make it. Period.

So much for my scouting acumen.

I jumped to these conclusions after seeing Richards play live for the first time, at the 2000 World Junior Hockey Championship in Skelleftea, Sweden. Richards was then a member of the Rimouski Océanic, and it's not like he wasn't ripping up the Quebec Major Junior Hockey League (QMJHL) that year. By season's end, Richards led the QMJHL in goals (71), assists (115), and points (186). He led the Océanic to the QMJHL championship and topped it off by winning the Memorial Cup. Oh, did I mention he was the Canadian Hockey League's player of the year and Memorial Cup MVP?

But putting up big numbers in the "Q" or any junior league doesn't mean your ticket gets punched to star in the NHL, and in fairness, my instant evaluation was based on seeing him play only seven games for Canada in dark and frigid northern Sweden, where Canada scored a 4–3 shootout win over the United States to win the bronze medal. (Yeah, that's it, lack of sunshine; that's what led me down the wrong path on Richards. You buying that? That's what I thought.)

There were plenty of guys on that team I figured were locks to play in the NHL and good bets to be stars. Richards, with one goal and one assist in seven games, wasn't one of them.

Dany Heatley was. Michael Ryder, too. And you knew the two sixteen-year-olds who hardly played—Jason Spezza and Jay Bouwmeester—would be making their mark one day.

Based on the 2000 World Junior Hockey Championship alone, Richards struck me as a nice player. Not overly big and not overly fast, but not a bad player by any means. But if a smallish forward was going to make it, Brandon Reid, who had four goals and nine points in seven games, looked like he had a dynamic quality to him that would serve him well in the NHL. Mind you, Richards did look to be an effective power play quarterback and I say that only to note that I got something right on this kid.

Well, so much for my scouting report. Reid never caught on as an NHL regular, although it was interesting to see him back as a depth role player with the Vancouver Canucks late in the 2006–07 season after years of playing in Europe.

As for Richards? In the meantime, all he did was go on to lead the Tampa Bay Lightning to the 2004 Stanley Cup, win the Conn Smythe Trophy as playoff MVP, establish himself as one of the NHL's great clutch players of all time (an NHL record seven game-winning goals in one playoff year), and sign a contract that makes him one of the highest-paid players in the NHL. Oh yeah, he also won the 2004 World Cup and was Canada's leading scorer at the 2006 Winter Olympics.

He has proven to be one of the most durable players in the NHL, rarely missing games. He plays more minutes than just about any forward in the NHL. He is one of the smartest players, one of the game's best playmakers. He is a terrific penalty killer. A great power play quarterback. A tremendous faceoff specialist. Simply put, he is one of the most complete players in the NHL today and even now he probably doesn't get the attention he deserves because there is an understated elegance to all that he does.

Now, not thinking Richards would be a big-time NHL star should never be confused with not wanting him to be one. He's a good kid from a good family and that was immediately apparent. If there were an award given to the outstanding parents of the Canadian players at the 2000 World Junior Hockey Championships, Brad's mom and dad, Delite and Glen, would have won it hands down.

It was like the Murray Harbour, Prince Edward Island, Chamber of Commerce had landed in northern Sweden. You could always tell when Delite and Glen had been through the hotel lobby in Skelleftea because the screen saver on the hotel lobby computer was adorned with a lovely overhead shot of beautiful Murray Harbour. Delite and Glen were everywhere, enjoying every minute of the experience. They are great ambassadors for their province, their community, and their family. Nicer people you will not meet.

Of course, the same thing can be said for Paul Hollingsworth, my colleague at TSN who has written the book you have in your hands. The Richards–Hollingsworth tandem is terrific. The former has a great story to tell, the latter a great ability to tell a story.

As for me, I am flattered, if not embarrassed, to have been asked to contribute in some small way.

But I feel better now. A true confession will always do that.

—Bob McKenzie

Acknowledgements

I AM MOST GRATEFUL TO SANDRA MCINTYRE AND HER NIMBUS COLLEAGUES FOR HAVING THE CONFIDENCE IN ME TO TACKLE THIS PROJECT. SPECIAL THANKS ALSO TO PATRICK MURPHY AND HEATHER BRYAN FOR THEIR EDITORIAL SUPPORT.

As for the people I interviewed, the list is long and my gratitude runs deep, because in the end they enabled me to get the job done. Brad, Delite, and Glen Richards did not know me before this project, and for that matter we're still not well acquainted. But after a few phone calls and emails I would like to think we developed a level of mutual trust that made this book possible. Without the help of the Richards family, there would be no book—it's that simple.

I would also like to thank Terry O'Malley, Terry McGarry, and the entire staff at Athol Murray College of Notre Dame. They always took my calls and they supplied me with great insight and terrific pictures from Brad's days in Wilcox.

Also, special thanks to Wayne Gretzky, John Tortorella, Craig Ramsay, Stan Butler, Jay Preble, Rick Dudley, Steve Ludzik, Thatcher Bell, Doris Labonté, Shawn MacKenzie, Gord Miller, Bob McKenzie, Don Koharski, and Pat Morris. They all have busy schedules but were eager to make a contribution.

My full time job is reporting for CTV/TSN. It's the kind of place where everyone is a king but no one wears a crown. We are a team and the following people are my bosses, co-workers, and above all else, my friends. Jay Witherbee, Mike Elgie, Mark Milliere, Jim Panousis, Steve Argintaru, Wade Keller, Steve Murphy, Jon Hynes, Leo Carter, Dean Willers, Paul Hemming, Peter Mallette, Marc Malette, and Greg Sands have all helped me over the years and given me the opportunity to grow professionally. I can't find the words to express my gratitude and loyalty in full measure. But "thank you" seems like a good start.

Finally, where would I be in life without my wife, Tamara? There was a time back in university when she would read the books from my English courses so she could best assist me in writing term papers. Fast-forward fifteen years, and during her maternity leave she was always busy pre-reading my manuscript, providing feedback and editorial insight. Tamara is my first editor in everything I do, and she's also my cherished companion in life. A wonderful wife, a loving mother, she's the best person I know and I'm lucky to be with her.

—Paul Hollingsworth

Introduction

Like many regions in Canada, the Maritimes have been forced to deal with "brain drain" — the migration of some of our most highly educated and skilled workforce. For some, leaving is a form of conventional wisdom, a gateway to a dream, an opportunity to put oneself on what could be a fast track to success. It happens in the professional world, and it happens in the sports world.

In 1979, for example, Al MacInnis left his home in Port Hood, Nova Scotia, to chase his hockey dream. The reason was simple: he needed to place himself in a more competitive environment—an environment conducive to growth and skill enhancement. It worked. After junior hockey stops in Regina and Kitchener, MacInnis would play in 1,416 regular season NHL games and 144 playoff games, and win a Stanley Cup with the Calgary Flames in 1989 while being named Conn Smythe Trophy winner as the playoffs' most valuable player. He would

cap his career accolades with a Norris Trophy in 1998–99 as the NHL's top defenceman. Leaving Nova Scotia was an enormous gamble, and the payoff was an opportunity to fully showcase his talents at a level of excellence while achieving a lifetime's worth of fame and fortune.

It's a model that Sidney Crosby of Cole Harbour, Nova Scotia, would also follow. Crosby was just fifteen years old in the autumn of 2002 and coming to the obvious conclusion that the Nova Scotia Major Midget Hockey League was no longer presenting enough of a challenge. Crosby left Nova Scotia for Faribault, Minnesota, where he enrolled at Shattuck–St. Mary's School to play for the school's hockey team. One season, 162 points, and a national high school championship later, Crosby was a household name. By 2006 he was being hailed as a future NHL superstar—and by some estimates he has already reached that status.

So here we see it. Two young, immensely talented hockey players leave home early, eventually coming away from the experience prepared to take the next step in their journey toward reaching the National Hockey League. Although the odds are long, it's the path that has been chosen by hundreds of other young Maritime hockey players, including Brad Richards, a minor hockey player from Murray Harbour, Prince Edward Island.

PREVIOUS PAGE: Murray Harbour, Prince Edward Island. Population: 357.

FACING PAGE: By Christmas of 1981, Brad already looked like he had found his calling.

BEGINNINGS

BRAD RICHARDS WAS BORN MAY 2, 1980, THE SON OF DELITE AND GLEN RICHARDS, THE LATTER A FORMER JUNIOR HOCKEY GOALIE. WHEN BRAD WAS JUST TWO-AND-A-HALF YEARS OLD, GLEN PUT HIS SON IN SKATES FOR THE FIRST TIME. "BRAD STEPPED ONTO THE ICE AND JUST TOOK OFF. HE TOOK RIGHT TO IT. HE HAD HIS STRIDE FROM THE START," SAID GLEN. "HE WAS ALWAYS WANTING TO GO TO THE RINK AND WHEN THE TIME WAS OVER HE NEVER WANTED TO GET OFF. HE PRETTY MUCH GREW UP ON THE ICE."

By his own accounts, Brad rarely left the ice during his early years. For reasons that are mostly linked to his passion for hockey and the island's small population, he played a lot and developed rapidly. "We were always practising," said Richards. "And usually there were only ten or eleven players on the hockey teams I played on, so we got lots of ice time." In time he became one of the top minor hockey players in the Prince Edward Island Hockey Association. Fellow Murray Harbour native Thatcher Bell grew up with Richards, and in addition to enjoying a lifelong friendship, the pair also played

together for two seasons in Rimouski in the Quebec Major Junior Hockey League (QMJHL). Bell remembers Richards being a dominant minor hockey player, but not like Sidney Crosby or Eric Lindros, two players who developed a reputation for being prolific scorers at a young age. "Obviously he was one of the best players on Prince Edward Island when we were younger," said Bell. "But I can't recall him getting seven or eight points per game. But he was always good—very good—and maybe the best for his age. He was always the leading scorer in any league right up until he left PEI."

him from his parents and his sister, Paige, not to mention Murray Harbour, the only home he had ever known. But it would also prove to be a fast-track mechanism—a tipping point in the life of a raw, talented hockey player.

"Leaving PEI and going to Notre Dame was the thing that got everything moving for him," said Glen. "I always talk about the sacrifices Brad has made in his life. He was fourteen, and he left his friends, he left his family, but he had a goal in mind, and he left."

Within weeks it was decided he would leave home and enroll at Athol Murray College of Notre Dame. Not yet fifteen years old, Brad Richards headed to an elite prep school on the other side of the country to play hockey for the Notre Dame Hounds.

At a very young age, and at times coached by his father, Glen, Brad searched for opportunities to further his hockey development. One vehicle that enhanced his on-ice capabilities was the Andrews Hockey Growth Program—a PEI-based summer hockey school put on by Allan Andrews that boasts seventeen graduates who have gone on to play in the NHL. While attending the hockey school, Brad and his family learned about a hockey program at a private school located in Wilcox, Saskatchewan.

As one of the top minor hockey players in Prince Edward Island, Brad needed to consider leaving the Island in order to further enhance his skills. While leaving the Island would prove to be fortuitous, it would also prove painful. It would remove

HEADING WEST

In Saskatchewan, if you drive half an hour south of Regina, you come to the town of Wilcox. A small dot on the prairie map, Wilcox is home to two hundred people, three grain elevators, one hockey rink, and an elite private school, Athol Murray College of Notre Dame, home to the Notre Dame Hounds hockey team.

To call Notre Dame a "hockey factory" would be unfair because the school boasts a decades-long commitment to academics. But to be sure, many young, skilled hockey players have attended the school to gain much-needed attention from American universities offering full athletic scholarships or from major junior teams in the Canadian Hockey League.

In 1980 the school enjoyed its shining moment on the silver screen when the feature movie, *The Hounds of Notre Dame*, was released in Canadian theatres. The film was nominated for nine Genie Awards (winning one, for best actor) in 1981 and its main storyline did more than depict the life of the institution's founder, Athol Murray—it helped to make Notre Dame itself a semi-household name in Canada.

Future NHL superstars have been groomed at Notre Dame. In 1988 goaltender Curtis Joseph and forward Rod Brind'Amour led the Hounds as they captured the Centennial Cup as Canada's top junior A hockey team. It was the high-water mark for the school. Brind'Amour and Joseph, after playing at Michigan State University and the University of Wisconsin, respectively, later went on to star in the NHL. Notre Dame suddenly became synonymous with hockey excellence in Canada. In the 1980s Russ Courtnall, Wendel Clark, and Gary Leeman were linemates on the Maple Leafs and all three were graduates of Notre Dame. Whether it was in the local Toronto media or on Hockey Night in Canada broadcasts, for a time the term "Hound Line" was part of the vernacular of Leafs Nation. In the decades since, the school has been seen as an ideal destination for talented young hockey players. It was the perfect destination for a fourteen-year-old who had outgrown Prince Edward Island's minor hockey system.

Brad Richards was the son of a prosperous third-generation lobster fisherman and his parents wanted their son to see the world, develop his hockey talent, and get an education. They also realized early in their son's life that lobster fishing was not going to be his career of choice. "Brad always liked skating on the water in the winter, but he didn't like going out on the water to fish," joked his father Glen. "I used to always say to him 'Get an education,' because I knew that he didn't want to be out there fishing." When the Richards family learned about the hockey program and educational opportunities

at Notre Dame, they decided that heading to Wilcox was the best possible course for Brad to take. The plan was simple: graduate from high school in Wilcox and earn a U.S. college scholarship. Reaching the NHL was not necessarily the main objective—developing Brad's talent was. If, in the end, Brad failed to fulfill his professional hockey dream and played in the NCAA instead, he would at least be equipped with an excellent post-secondary education. In short, the thought was to trade hockey for education, with an eye on pursuing a career that did not include lobster fishing on the Atlantic Ocean.

Leaving home for the first time is never easy. Leaving home at age fourteen to play hockey at a boarding school 4,200 kilometres away was a sacrifice as well as a tremendous psychological challenge for a young man who had spent his entire life with his family in the sheltered world of Murray Harbour. Richards recalls questioning whether he was making the right decision.

PREVIOUS PAGE: Notre Dame students and staff gather to cheer on Brad and Vincent Lecavalier, two of the school's most famous alumni, during the 2004 Stanley Cup playoffs.

RIGHT: The Richards family in 2001. From left: Glen, Delite, Paige, and Brad.

These pangs of doubt were on his mind even as he prepared to leave home for the first time.

"It was very hard," recalled Richards. "I didn't really know how big the decision was. There was a couple of times where I broke down crying not sure if I wanted to go. Looking back, I was too young to really know what was going on."

When the move finally came and he was left on his own for the first time in his life, Richards's fears about being so far away from home were realized. He remembers the early days at Notre Dame as being particularly painful and lonely. It was a tough time for a teenager who admittedly had always been close to his family. "The first week was very tough," Richards said. "I was crying or close to crying every morning when I woke up, but once all the roommates got up and we went to school, it was fine."

Notre Dame coach Terry O'Malley hands out schedules to the bantam AAA team. Brad is in the grey ball cap and Vincent Lecavalier is seated to his right.

Brad's parents knew at the time that their son was facing his first big challenge as an adolescent, but they did not know the full depth of his despair. "We didn't find out until the next year how hard it was for him and by then the school had really grown on him," said Glen. Having Brad leave home brought many moments of second-guessing for Glen and Delite. "It was terrible, just terrible," recalled Glen. "We never went through this before...it was like losing my right arm. Some nights we would wonder if we had made a mistake. When I was kid going to camp for few days were more than I could handle and I kept thinking about that, especially when he first left. But Brad was a mature fourteen, he was always positive and he never gave up."

In hindsight, allowing a teenage son to leave home to play hockey may seem to be the kind of decision a family would struggle with for a long time. However, for Brad's mom, the magnitude of the move wasn't fully felt until her son left Murray Harbour. "It was very hard, but it happened so quickly. One week it was decided that he was going to go, three weeks later he was gone. There was no time to dwell on it and say 'What are we doing?'"

As difficult as it was for Richards, he stayed and made sure that he upheld his commitment to Notre Dame. "I never really came close to saying 'I wanna come home,'" he said.

Brad with a teenaged Lecavalier in 1994. The two became fast friends off the ice and excellent players on it.

Not only did Notre Dame grow on Richards, but he would, in short time, prove to be a perfect fit for the school, securing his place as one of the school's all-time top players. But his head coach wasn't sold on his ability, at least not at first. Terry O'Malley spent twenty-three years coaching the Hounds' bantam, midget, and junior teams and recalled his first impression of the fourteen-year-old. "I wondered if he was going to make it," O'Malley said. "His size and skating weren't as strong as others, but he had the ability to put the puck in the net and in many ways that set him apart. Still, I wasn't sure at first. Then people kept saying to me 'Keep in mind he's only first-year bantam,' so I decided to stay with him. Over time he developed such a strong command of the ice."

Looking back on his Notre Dame years, Brad still credits O'Malley with having had a tremendous impact on him —an impact that was felt both on the ice and away from the hockey arena. "Terry O'Malley is a great man and was a great coach," said Richards. "He had great ideas about hockey but even better ones about how to grow up and be a good person. He always kept an eye on me on and off the ice. He had the credentials of a pro coach but we had him as bantam and midget players, so we were very fortunate. We still talk, and he will leave me a message once in a while with little reminders [about my play]. He is a great person."

Playing on Notre Dame's bantam team for the first two seasons, Richards averaged a point per game and played alongside a teenager from Montreal named Vincent Lecavalier. The two were roommates and O'Malley remembers the two young men developing an instant bond. "Right from the

Minor hockey's age divisions

Hockey Canada recognizes six divisions of minor hockey. In some cases underage players are allowed to play in older age divisions, but it typically takes a peewee player seven years to advance through the minor hockey system before reaching the junior division.

Junior:	18–19 years old
Midget:	15–17 years old
Bantam:	13–14 years old
Peewee:	11–12 years old
Atom:	9–10 years old
Novice:	8 years old
Pre-novice:	7 years old or younger

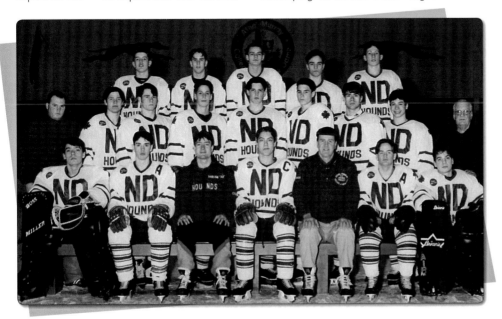

The 1994–95 bantam AAA Notre Dame Hounds. Brad is in the back row, far left.

Terry O'Malley presenting Brad with the SJHL's rookie of the year award in 1997.

get-go, they were fast friends," recalls O'Malley. "I remember they were always outside playing ball hockey in the frigid cold in their spare time. When you have the kind of talent these two have, it's not just what you do in practice so much as what you do in your spare time. They were both young and in the same situation and in time they became like brothers. He roomed with Vince and they both helped each other a lot."

Glen also remembers the two young teenagers developing a close relationship from the outset of their time together with the Hounds—a relationship that helped them mature together as they approached adulthood. "They are and always have been like brothers. They were away together, both lonely and both sort of feeding off each other. They quickly developed a brotherly level of companionship and even competition. They'll always have a special relationship because of what they went through during those early years."

For any fourteen-year-old, having a close friend is crucial, but for Brad, it was even more important. Richards recalls meeting Lecavalier and agrees with his father's assessment that not only was it the beginning of a strong friendship, but that bonding with his new friend at such a crucial juncture was perhaps the most significant aspect of their relationship. "Vinny and I became close friends very quickly. We lived in the same room with the same corner bunks; we were...the only ninth graders on the bantam AAA team, so we were together all the time. It really helped to have a close friend. We had a lot of the same interests. We both went through the good and bad together which made it easier to get by."

The pair soon began their rapid ascent within the Notre Dame hockey program. In the 1994–95 and 1995–96 seasons Richards and Lecavalier were called up to Notre Dame's midget hockey team for the playoffs and both made significant contributions against players one and two years older. "Brad was quarterbacking the power play for the midget team as a bantam-aged player when we called him up for the playoffs," said O'Malley. "At fifteen he could pass and find people on the ice, especially if someone would get out of position. He also had a shot like a cannon."

After two years as teammates, it was time for Lecavalier to move on while Richards was

Best Friends

In the words of Delite Richards, "They are like brothers. It's quite special to see." Rimouski Océanic head coach Doris Labonté was more poetic when he explained, "They are like fingers on the same hand." Brad Richards and Vincent Lecavalier appear to be linked together for life. From roommates at Notre Dame, to Rimouski in the QMJHL, Tampa Bay in the NHL, to Team Canada and Ak-Bars in Russia, these two young men appear destined to remain friends and, just maybe, always teammates.

Like brothers, they also share a spirit of competition. "They are very competitive with one another," says Lightning head coach John Tortorella. "I think they have a special care for each other, but from my perspective these two guys also push each other on the ice and in life. It's great to see and it's also great for our team."

Brad Richards and Vincent Lecavalier in 1994: new roommates at Notre Dame.

moving up. In 1996–97, Vincent Lecavalier said goodbye to Wilcox to lace up for the Rimouski Océanic of the Quebec Major Junior Hockey League. In his first season in northern Quebec, Lecavalier was a rookie sensation for the Océanic, finishing with 103 points and being named the Canadian Hockey League's rookie of the year. Richards stayed back at Notre Dame and joined the junior team, even though he was only the age of a typical first-year midget player. In his one season in the Saskatchewan Junior Hockey League, he totaled eighty-seven points in sixty-three games while being named rookie of the year. After his third season at Notre Dame, the young Maritimer was already prepared to take on a new challenge. It was a time to leave, a time to advance, and a time to begin the next chapter of his fledgling hockey career. "I knew we were going to miss him," says O'Malley as he reflects on Richards's departure from Wilcox. "But we sure were proud of watching this fine young man move on to a new level."

When Richards left home at age fourteen, the goal was to secure a scholarship at an American university. Looking back, O'Malley admits that initially the college goal was the most realistic one for Richards based on his size and skating ability. An NHL contract was not yet on the radar. "When he first came, I thought he would one day become a great college player," said O'Malley. "But he worked hard to improve and I was wrong."

RISING STAR

WITH SUCCESS AT NOTRE DAME CAME A CHANGE IN DIRECTION. RICHARDS HAD DEVELOPED HIS PLAY TO THE POINT WHERE HE BEGAN TO GARNER ATTENTION FROM THE MAJOR JUNIOR HOCKEY COMMUNITY IN CANADA. THE ATTENTION LED TO A NEW TRACK IN HIS HOCKEY CAREER.

Instead of pursuing a path that included trading his hockey talents for an education, at age seventeen he rejoined Lecavalier to play in a city just an eight-hour drive from Murray Harbour. In the 1997 QMJHL midget draft, Richards was the seventh overall pick and the top selection by the Océanic—a selection that, according to his former bantam coach, was partly the work of Lecavalier himself. "Vince told the Océanic staff to check out this Richards kid at Notre Dame," said O'Malley. "One day, a group from the Rimouski team came out here to watch him play and the next thing you know, Brad was going to the Océanic."

Playing for the Océanic meant Richards was also begin-

ning a new path in his hockey career. By choosing the QMJHL, Brad was now opening the door for a possible career as a professional hockey player. "I never thought playing in the NHL was possible when I left for Notre Dame," said Richards. "My main goal was always to get an education at a U.S. school on a scholarship. Going to Rimouski meant I would start playing with players who had been drafted or were about to be drafted. It was around then, when I was seventeen or eighteen years old, that playing in the NHL became a goal of mine."

Richards confirmed his former coach's recollection of the circumstances surrounding his move to Rimouski, taking

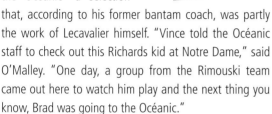

1996-97 Notre Dame Regular Season Statistics	
Games	63
Goals	39
Assists	48
Points	87

it a step further by crediting Lecavalier with single-handedly arranging for Rimouski to pursue and then draft him. "Vinny was the biggest part of getting me to Rimouski," recalls Richards. "He called me at Notre Dame and asked if I would like to go there. Rimouski had asked Vinny to feel me out about the [QMJHL] draft and about being an English player in a French town. From there they contacted my family and it all went forward. But without Vinny being there I never would have went."

But the man pulling the strings to make it all happen wasn't Lecavalier, O'Malley, or even Richards himself. It was Océanic head coach Doris Labonté who sent his scouts to Saskatchewan to see Richards play. It was a move that made Labonté's decision easy heading into that spring's draft. "Brad was unknown. An unknown player playing in a place far away," he said. "We sent two guys to Notre Dame to see him and they told us because he was already playing junior A [hockey] he would for sure become an impact player for us. Vinny [Lecavalier] was also saying it. So one plus one equalled two and we did the right thing and brought Brad to Rimouski." For the second time in three years, Brad Richards was on the move. This time he was travelling back east, much closer to home.

In the weeks leading up their scheduled reunion in Rimouski, Richards and Lecavalier unexpectedly found themselves back together on the ice to play in the Three Nations Cup in the Czech Republic. In August of 1997 Richards donned

PREVIOUS PAGE: Brad and Vincent with Océanic coach Doris Labonté in 2003.

RIGHT: Brad and teammates after capturing the 1997 Three Nations Cup.

Canada's red-and-white uniform for the first time in his young career when, with several future NHLers, he was selected to Canada's under-eighteen hockey team. Being selected to the team came as a surprise for Richards.

"I was playing tier two [junior A] and was selected with guys that were playing major junior," Richards said. "It was a great time and I have some great memories. Just putting on the jersey and the whole Team Canada experience was amazing. We won gold so that made it even better."

Stan Butler, who would later serve as head coach for Canada's national junior team, was an assistant that year for the under-eighteen team and remembers Richards as a young, raw, and largely untested player in the summer of 1997. "He was young, still growing, and still developing, and here he was playing alongside future NHLers like Simon Gagne, Mike Ribeiro, and Vinny Lecavalier. He was also playing junior A when many of his Team Canada teammates were major junior players," said Butler. "But he had a high skill level, and he was also used to playing with Vinny. That helped him a lot from a comfort level and I wouldn't be surprised if his experiences at that tournament served him well in the future."

Reunited with Lecavalier in his first year with the Océanic, Richards soared. Playing in ten more regular season games than Lecavalier, Richards finished the regular season with 115 points, tied for fifth in the league with, who else, Lecavalier—a performance good enough

to earn him a roster spot in the 1998 QMJHL All-star Game. Unlike Lecavalier, who had won the RDS Trophy as the QMJHL Rookie of the Year in his first season in Rimouski just a year earlier, Richards finished second in total points among rookies, behind Mike Ribeiro from the Rouyn–Noranda Huskies, who tallied 125 points. That first season in Rimouski, Richards also began what would soon become a career trend by excelling in the post-season. In nineteen playoff games with the Océanic, he scored eight goals while adding twenty-four assists—third best on the team.

Richards had by no means returned home, but playing hockey in the eastern portion of the country did allow his family to be together more than in the previous three years. "It was still a ways away," said Glen. "But it was better. You can't jump in a plane and head off to Wilcox anytime you want. We would get out there two or three times a year at best. But Rimouski is only a seven- or eight-hour drive from home. Pretty soon we were going every weekend and we went back and forth a lot. It was still far, but compared to Notre Dame it was like having him next door."

Delite also appreciated the Quebec culture and the new environment of which her son was now a part. "It was more like home," said Delite. "When we were flying into Rimouski it was like we were flying into the Maritimes."

Playing in a new province not only brought with it an immersion into a new culture, but it was also a chance to learn a new language,

Brad, Phil Esposito, and Vincent Lecavalier at the 1998 NHL entry draft.

and Richards caught on quickly when it came to speaking French. Within months he was successfully doing interviews with French reporters, although he downplays his linguistic abilities today. "I never knew much French until I went to Rimouski," says Richards. "The first year was very hard but after that I realized that I was understanding everything. I became comfortable and started to try to talk to people. Halfway through my second year I was able to do some interviews. I could never speak it perfectly but got by okay for the most part."

Delite felt that having her son live in a French province and learn the language was a chance to experience a new way of life and in doing so, gain an invaluable life skill. She felt that, as an English teenager, Brad needed to at least make an earnest attempt at the language, if

for no other reason than to earn the respect of his teammates and Océanic fans. "I thought by Christmas he was doing fine," said Delite. "He tried and that was important. By learning to speak French, that helped [the fans and his teammates] accept him."

Doris Labonté agreed that "learning French didn't hurt Brad one bit. It gave his fans extra reason to support him and cheer for him." It also would be a life skill he brought with him to the NHL as he continued to conduct live interviews on French language hockey broadcasts.

In June of 1998, the Tampa Bay Lightning selected Vincent Lecavalier first overall in the NHL's entry draft. The Lightning did not have a second-round pick, but when Richards was still available in the third round, Tampa Bay chose him with the sixty-fourth pick of the draft. In time, grabbing Richards in the third round would prove to be a steal for Tampa Bay. Through the 2005–06 season, nine players selected before Richards had not yet made it to the NHL.

Brad's father remembers the thrill of seeing his son being selected, but at the time he also cautioned Brad to be realistic about his long-term chances of reaching the NHL. "I used to say to Brad, getting drafted is just a step," said Glen. "I saw it as a small step, an important step, but just a step. He knew he still had to work hard."

Seeing her son called to the podium and then pull on a Tampa Bay Lightning jersey was, for Delite, the culmination of four years of hard work and sacrifice. "It was like a dream," said Delite. "It was a very big thrill for all of us, especially Brad. He deserved everything he got. To leave home so young, he went through so much. We were all so pleased to see this happen to him."

While growing up, Richards cheered for the Chicago Blackhawks. By coincidence, former Blackhawks goaltender Tony Esposito was the assistant general manager for the Lightning, working for his brother Phil, the general manager. As pleased as Richards was about being selected by an NHL team, being picked alongside Lecavalier and by the Esposito brothers added to the once-in-a-lifetime thrill. "I had never thought about Tampa Bay. I was just happy to be drafted to the NHL," said Richards. "It was a bonus that it was once again with Vinny. Phil and Tony Esposito drafted me so it

was a thrill for me and my family to meet those two guys at the draft."

Being drafted by the same NHL team was a remarkable turn of events and a fortunate circumstance for two young men who not only enjoyed an off-ice friendship, but who were fast developing an on-ice chemistry also. If everything went as planned, Lecavalier and Richards would one day play alongside one another in the NHL. It was also fortunate happenstance, as the Lightning had the first overall pick and sixty-fourth pick only through trades. If not for those deals, the two players could have gone to different teams.

However, the Lightning decided Richards needed to play at least two more years of junior hockey before jumping to the professional ranks. Lecavalier was a different matter. A first-overall draft selection, the eighteen-year-old was being fast-tracked into a premature entrance into the NHL. He was on the move to sunny Florida and once again far away from his friend and teammate.

The Rimouski Océanic came into existence in 1995–96, when the St. Jean Lynx moved their operations there. While the QMJHL has developed a reputation as a solid training ground for future NHL stars, it has also been beset by franchise instability. Three teams the Lynx played against in 1989 (Trois Rivières Draveurs, Longueuil College-Français, and Granby Bisons), for example, would no longer be in existence by 1995. But by relocating, rather than folding, the Lynx franchise found stability. Maurice Tanguay, along with a local consortium of deep-pocketed owners, bought the team and a major junior hockey success story was born.

In their first season at the Rimouski Coliseum, the Océanic performed not unlike an expansion team, finishing with just fifty-four points, in tenth place in the fourteen-team QMJHL. In the franchise's second year of existence, Rimouski drafted Lecavalier, and along with forwards Eric Normandin, Eric Belanger, and defenceman Derrick Walser, the team soared to thirty-four wins, seventy-four points and a fourth-place finish in their division. By the time the 1998–99 season rolled around, the Océanic were evolving into a QMJHL force. While Lecavalier had jumped to the NHL, Richards stayed behind and put together two of the best offensive seasons in league history.

Now playing without his best friend, Richards improved his offensive output by sixteen points in his sophomore season and finished fourth in the league in regular season scoring. Once again Richards was a dominant force in the post-season, totaling twenty-one points in eleven games. It was around this time that his father began to see his son as a future NHL player. "When he went to Notre Dame we were thinking this will get Brad an education," said Glen. "That was the goal, so I always thought in terms of him playing junior or university hockey. Then he was drafted and began to play at such a high level. Toward the end of his second year in Rimouski I started to realize my son had a shot at playing in the NHL, but I knew he was still young and still had to keep working hard."

Like Glen, Delite had always envisioned the college route as the logical next step. But the draft and Brad's determination helped change her thinking. "It was when everybody started talking about the draft," said Delite. "Up until that point he was always talking about university. But he kept working so hard and knowing that he would always work extra hard I started to see it differently. He was always like that and after a while I knew that effort could get him to the NHL."

A hockey insider was also sold on Richards's ability and recognized his tremendous upside. TSN's NHL play-by-play announcer Gord Miller watched Richards for the first time during the 1998–99 season and came away impressed by his ability and versatility. "At first he didn't stand out as a highly skilled player, but it wasn't too long before I thought 'This guy is unbelievable,'" said Miller. "He was productive everywhere. He could pass, he was a playmaker, and he was strong on the power play. You could just see that this guy had character and was on his way to doing great things."

With two years under his belt, the soon-to-be-nineteen-year-old had established himself as a young man with a limitless hockey future. His on-ice accomplishments in many ways mirrored that of his team. Both were young and developing quickly and both were displaying clear indicators that they were on the cusp of great success.

Hockey has witnessed many dream seasons. Take, for example, the 1975–76 Montreal Canadiens. That season Montreal lost just eleven regular season games en route to their seventeenth

Brad Richards in flight against the United States at the 2000 IIHF World Junior Hockey Championship.

Stanley Cup. In 1981–82, Wayne Gretzky scored an NHL record 92 goals and added 120 assists. Fast forward to 2004–05, when seventeen-year-old Sidney Crosby won his second consecutive CHL Player of the Year Award after totalling 168 points in just 62 regular season games. These seasons are all the result of spectacular individual and team successes—seasons where things fall into place and everything seems to be working. Brad Richards's 1999–2000 season was one of those campaigns. When the season started, he was just another young NHL draftee with a bright future. By the time the season was over, Richards would secure his place in the history books as one of the greatest QMJHL players of all time.

Looking back on Richards's performance in the 1999–2000 campaign, Océanic head coach Doris Labonté says the drive displayed by his young forward had its roots in the NHL preseason. Not unlike other NHL draftees, Richards had attended the Lightning training camp at the beginning of the season. It was a chance to experience some high-calibre competition, but unlike the 1998 camp, he did not get a chance to play in any preseason games—a slight that left him frustrated and anxious to prove himself during the upcoming junior season. "The day he came back from his camp with Tampa Bay he was not happy. He was left out of the exhibition games and he didn't like it, not a bit," said Labonté. "From then on he was on a mission to prove something. It was incredible to watch his drive from that tough

moment. He knew he could do something, but he had to prove it to others."

In 1999–2000, the Océanic were poised to make a run at a QMJHL championship. Given their relatively short history, competing for the league title in just their fifth year of operation was in itself an impressive accomplishment. Led by Richards, fellow Islander Thatcher Bell, Juraj Kolnik, and Jean-Phillipe Cadieux, the Océanic were fast out of the gate. Within weeks it became evident Rimouski would be the dominant force during the regular season—a regular season in which they would lead the league with 48 victories and 102 points.

It was a dream season in the making and this was Richards's team. He led the team and the league in every significant offensive category—71 goals, 115 assists, and 186 points. It was a stunning performance and one of the most successful regular seasons in the history of the Quebec Major Junior Hockey League (in fact, it was the highest QMJHL point total since Yanic Perreault of Trois-Rivières scored 185 points in 1990–91). But what made Richards's success even more impressive was the fact that he played in just sixty-three games, the result of missing most of the month of December to skate with Canada's entry in the 2000 IIHF World Junior Hockey Championship.

Being named a member of the Canadian junior hockey team in December was a special moment for Richards. He and the rest of his new teammates were off to Skelleftea and Umea, Sweden, attempting to end Canada's two-year gold medal drought. That didn't happen as Canada finished a disappointing third, but playing for head coach Claude Julien, who had also coached Richards at the 1997 Three Nations Cup, Richards contributed offensively, finishing with one goal and one assist in seven games played. "The world junior tournament is something we all watched as a family at Christmas," said Richards. "It was a great honour to be able to go to that tournament."

Beyond the frustration of having to settle for a third-place finish, the experience brought many positives for the entire Richards family, a family that had been fractured by Richards's travels to Wilcox and Rimouski. The 2000 junior tournament was an opportunity for the family to spend the holidays together overseas. "Northern Sweden at Christmas was special. We got a bronze and as you know that is not enough as a Canadian player, but when I look back, it was still nice to at least get a medal," recalled Richards. "I played with some great players and my parents were there, which did make it even more special. That was the first time they were overseas, so seeing a new country was also exciting for them and for me."

Delite Richards remembers the occasion as more than a typical hockey tournament. It was a chance to see her son play alongside the top teenage players in the world, while forging new relationships with the other Canadian families who also travelled to Sweden. "The hockey was special and so was our time with Brad, but it was also neat to spend the time and share the experience with other families."

FACING PAGE: Competing at the junior championship in Sweden, Richards and Team Canada settled for a bronze medal.

As disappointing as the bronze medal finish was, within several months Richards would wipe away those frustrating memories by capturing junior hockey's top prize while walking away from his junior career with a staggering number of single-season awards. "When he came back it was like he was taking the next step, like he now had something to prove," said Delite. "Brad's determination, like it has at other times in life, carried him the rest of the season."

Rather than talk about his individual performance, Richards reflects on 1999–2000 as a team accomplishment—a team that in his opinion was almost unbeatable during the regular season, especially after Christmas. "We had a great year," said Richards. "Our team had it all and we just knew we were going to win. We were looked at as a great offensive team, but I think we had everything. Our record was like forty-nine and zero when leading after two periods. So that gives you an idea of how confident we were as a team, not only as individuals."

MEMORIAL CUP 2000

BRAD RICHARDS AND THE OCÉANIC STORMED INTO THE POST-SEASON WITH MOMENTUM AND THEIR EYES FIXED ON A BERTH IN THE 2000 MEMORIAL CUP TO BE HELD IN HALIFAX—A MARITIME HOCKEY FIRST. TO GET THERE, THEY WOULD HAVE TO WIN THEIR LEAGUE TITLE. IT TOOK JUST TWELVE GAMES FOR RIMOUSKI TO DISPATCH ITS PLAYOFF OPPONENTS AND CAPTURE THE FRANCHISE'S FIRST LEAGUE CROWN. THE QMJHL-CHAMPION OCÉANIC HEADED INTO THE MEMORIAL CUP ON A ROLL, AND THE TOURNAMENT WAS TO BE HELD JUST A THREE-AND-A-HALF-HOUR DRIVE FROM THE RICHARDS HOME IN MURRAY HARBOUR.

Shawn MacKenzie, head coach of the host Halifax Mooseheads during the 2000 Memorial Cup, says Richards elevated his play that week to a historic level. "What impressed me most and where he may have been most dominant was his consistency to rise to the occasion in every game," said MacKenzie. "He never took a night off, he never took a period off, and he never took a shift off, [as] some of the game's great players sometimes do. In the second or third period in games that week, you could see by his actions on the ice he was saying to his coaches and teammates, 'Follow me and we'll get it done.' Well, he

did get it done and it was something to watch."

The Mooseheads turned some heads by winning their first two games at the tournament. As the host team and only non-conference champion in the four-team field, Halifax was not expected to be competitive. But back-to-back wins over Barrie and Kootenay by a combined score of 12–3 secured Halifax a berth in the semifinal. They would lose their rematch with the Barrie Colts 6–3, however, falling short in their quest to become the first Maritime-based team to win the Memorial Cup. In the end, the expected happened as Rimouski, prohibitive

Memorial Cup

The Memorial Cup is the championship of major junior hockey in North America. The trophy dates back to 1918 and for fifty-four years, teams competed for the Memorial Cup in a regional playoff format. In 1972, a round robin tournament was introduced featuring the champions of the Western Hockey League, the Ontario Hockey League, and the Quebec Major Junior Hockey League. In 1983, the Memorial Cup tournament was expanded to include a fourth team, the host of the tournament. All three major junior hockey leagues play under the umbrella organization called the Canadian Hockey League (CHL). Thus the Memorial Cup is often referred to as the championship trophy for the CHL (although Canadian major junior leagues do have American-based teams as well).

PREVIOUS PAGE: Richards and the Océanic entered the Memorial Cup as strong favourites. They would not disappoint.

FACING PAGE: Richards finished the Memorial Cup with ten points, tied for the lead in tournament scoring.

favourites coming into the eight-day tournament, won each of its games by at least two goals and captured its first Memorial Cup in franchise history.

From teammate and fellow Prince Edward Islander Thatcher Bell's point of view, Richards's statistics offered solid proof of how important he was to the team, and how dominant a player he had become in junior hockey. "As far as Brad's contribution and importance as a player all you need to do is look at his numbers," said Bell. "He won the league and CHL scoring race, playoff scoring race, and he was the leader on a championship team. We wanted to have Brad on the ice, especially in big games."

It was an incredibly successful week, and the perfect end to a storybook season. Rimouski defeated Barrie 6–2 in the championship final, with Richards scoring the first goal of the game at 3:07 of the second period. "In that final game we were in tough and there was no score," recalled Labonté. "He jumped over the boards and went out there and scored the goal. That's what good players and leaders do. It was like he was basically saying 'Follow me boys, we can do this.'"

Just as he had in the regular season and QMJHL playoffs, Richards led the Memorial Cup tournament in scoring (he finished tied for the lead) with four goals and six assists, helping his team reach the pinnacle of the Canadian junior hockey

world. And his scoring had actually increased during the post-season. During the regular season Richards's offensive output was 2.95 points per game. In the playoffs, he averaged 3.08 points, finishing with twenty-four assists and twenty-seven points overall—tops in the CHL. "Winning the Memorial Cup in Halifax was pretty special for me," Richards said. "Growing up in the Maritimes and playing a lot of tournaments as a kid there made it as close as it gets to being home."

On his way to the championship game, Richards had to deal with some unexpected adversity. The Barrie Colts, champions of the Ontario Hockey League (OHL), featured a talented but troubled forward, Mike Jefferson, who finished with 110 points in 83 regular season and playoff games. In the days leading into the final weekend at the Halifax Metro Centre, Jefferson told reporters Richards "wouldn't last five games" in the OHL. Then, after Rimouski's 6–2 championship win over Barrie, Jefferson shook every hand on the Rimouski team except Richards's. After the final game, Richards, who remained silent about the issue during the tournament, finally responded. "Sometimes you've got to watch what you say in the papers because it motivates the other team," Richards said immediately after the game as he took a break from the on-ice celebrations. "We've always been careful not to do that, but [Jefferson] motivated me and he motivated the team. We're a close team and when somebody trashes a player, everyone gets mad. He never shook my hand...that just shows what kind of guy he is."

Richards helped bring Rimouski its first-ever Memorial Cup.

As puzzling as Jefferson's behaviour was, it would also prove to be portentous. By the time he reached the NHL with the St. Louis Blues, his surname had been changed to Danton. Then, in 2004, just two days after the Blues were eliminated from the 2004 Stanley Cup playoffs, he was arrested following an FBI investigation of a murder-for-hire plot. In 2005, at the age of twenty-five, Mike Danton was sentenced to seven-and-a-half years in a United States prison.

As Danton began a descent that would see him behind bars, Richards was leaving junior hockey after three years on a trajectory that had him heading toward future NHL stardom. Having run away with the scoring title, Richards had also accumulated a lot of new hardware for his trophy case back in Murray Harbour. In his third and final season with the Océanic he had captured the Jean Béliveau Trophy as the regular season's top scorer, the Telus Cup as the QMJHL's Offensive Player of the Year, the Michel Brière Trophy as the league's most valuable player, and the Paul Dumont Trophy as the personality of the year—an award given to the top newsmaker during the regular season. Richards was also named QMJHL Player of the

At the end of his junior career, Richards walked away with the Jean Béliveau Trophy, the Telus Cup, the Michel Brière Trophy, the Paul Dumont Trophy, the Memorial Cup MVP award, and the CHL Player of the Year Award. Oh, and his team, the Rimouski Océanic, captured the Memorial Cup.

Brad and his parents with the Memorial Cup in 2000.

Month in October, January, and February. After eight days in Halifax he was named Memorial Cup tournament MVP and member of the first all-star team. Then, in the week following the Memorial Cup, Richards was named CHL Player of the Year while being recognized as the CHL's top scorer and winner of the best plus-minus rating.

Just barely twenty years old in June of 2000, Richards had finished a remarkable season. He had helped Canada's national junior team win

Brad with his Memorial Cup hardware and Egide Jean and Jean d'arc Jean, his hosts in Rimouski.

a bronze medal, led his Rimouski Océanic to its first President's Cup and Memorial Cup, and captured eleven individual CHL awards. But even with all of this success, he still did not have his name on an NHL contract. As he waited for his turn to hoist the Memorial Cup trophy, Richards took a moment to discuss his uncertain future: "I want to celebrate tonight and tomorrow, but when I get back to Rimouski, I'll be on the phone with my agent." His agent was Pat Morris, and the pair had serious matters to discuss with Tampa Bay Lightning general manager Rick Dudley—and time was running short.

When a player is selected in the NHL's entry draft the team has two years to sign him to a contract. If the player is not signed, he is eligible to re-enter the draft. On the morning of May 29, 2000, Brad Richards was suddenly a former junior hockey superstar without an NHL team. The Lightning had until the first of June—just seventy-two hours—to get a deal done or they would lose the rights to one of the most successful CHL players in a decade. "It will be a hectic three days," Richards said as he prepared to leave the Halifax Metro Centre. "Hopefully I'll get something done. If not, I'm not going to worry about it."

Meanwhile, Lightning general manager Rick Dudley was in a bind and was less than optimistic about the chances of having Richards's name on a contract. Having just completed its eighth season since entering the league through expansion in 1992, Tampa Bay had made the post-season just once, in 1995–96. But heading into training camp in the fall of 2000, the organization had begun to stockpile an impressive list of young players. Along with Lecavalier, the Lightning roster also boasted young forwards Martin St. Louis and Frederik Modin. All were part of a youth movement and were still at a point in their careers where their salaries were relatively reasonable. Dudley wouldn't be permitted to toss around a lot of money to sign a third-round draft pick, regardless of his junior exploits. Morris wanted Richards to sign for $975,000, but Dudley was holding out for a lower figure. With the clock ticking down, Dudley was not optimistic. "I don't hold out a lot of hope right now that we'll sign Brad Richards," Dudley said on May 30. "We've made a very significant offer and we're not going to set a precedent for how much we pay a third-round pick."

Today, Dudley speaks candidly about how badly he wanted Richards signed but says he was facing resistance from within the Lightning organization. "There were people below me and above me who did not want me to sign this kid," said Dudley. "I had followed Brad all through junior hockey and I kept saying 'We have to sign this kid.' One of my superiors asked me, 'Can you guarantee he will be a superstar?' I said I can't, but I can guarantee if we let him

go and he gets drafted by another team, we will look silly."

Although Dudley was convinced Richards would one day succeed in the NHL, the turning point came during the Memorial Cup in Halifax. He approached his unsigned draft pick outside of the Océanic dressing room—a typical hands-on approach for the former NHL player and head coach. Jay Feaster, who would eventually become Dudley's successor in Tampa Bay, admired his predecessor's work ethic when it came to evaluating hockey talent. "Rick is hockey 24-7, 365 days a year, any hour of the day or night," said Feaster. "I used to say to Rick that he's the kind of guy who hates to take two hours out of his hockey day on December twenty-fifth to open his presents." With Feaster's assessment in mind, it should come as no surprise that Dudley was in the Halifax Metro Centre, outside the Rimouski dressing room, waiting to challenge Richards in person.

"I was in Halifax and I went down under the stands before one of the games to say hello and not so subtly let him know I was watching him," says Dudley. "It was a test, a challenge, and [Richards] knew it. He knew what I was doing and why I was doing it. I wanted to see how he would respond, especially given his contract status. That night he scored something like three points, and that's when I knew this was a special young man."

Later that evening, following Rimouski's 7–2 victory, Dudley called Lightning head coach Steve Ludzik who was home for the off-season

Doris Labonté - Rimouski Océanic Head Coach

Doris Labonté has led the Rimouski Océanic to two President's Cups as Quebec Major Junior Hockey League champions, and two Memorial Cup finals appearances, winning the trophy in 2000. He's also had the opportunity to coach three junior players who have gone on to enjoy stardom in the NHL: Vincent Lecavalier, Sidney Crosby, and Brad Richards. Richards, however, is the one Labonté says he's most proud of—not because he likes him more than the others but because he believes Richards has had a harder time proving himself to people who suspected he lacked the tools requisite to play professional hockey.

"We're proud of all our former players. Some are in university and some are in the NHL," said Labonté. "I'm talking about some pretty big hockey names. But Brad wasn't supposed to do this, or at least that was according to the hockey experts. People said he wasn't strong. He wasn't fast. He was knock-kneed. They were wrong. Really wrong! I knew it and so did Brad, but he had to work hard to prove it and he did. I'm proud of his hockey sense, his motivation, and his personality away from the ice. For those reasons he's the player from Rimouski I'm most proud of."

Looking back on his junior career, Richards recognizes that Labonté, like Terry O'Malley at Notre Dame, had a profound impact on his career and life.

"Doris was a great coach and he really protected his players," said Richards. "I couldn't have asked for more. He used me in every situation and played me a lot and just let me grow as a player. Overall I think I have been successful early in my NHL career because of Rimouski and Doris. I had a great time there and a ton of ice time to let me become the player I was with the right teaching. I went into the NHL ready and confident."

Even six years after his protegé's junior career had ended, Labonté, ever the protective coach, was still anxious to point out that while Richards's 186 points and MVP awards set him apart from all other players in 2000, it was his defensive-minded play that proved even then that he could, and probably would, go on to have a successful NHL career. "The most important part of Brad's play was his plus-minus. We could be up 5–0, down 2–0, or scoreless, it didn't matter. He was always the top guy to have on the ice at all times. People see those 186 points and they may think he was a one-way player, a sniper. He wasn't."

in Ontario. Ludzik recalled his boss's reaction after Richards's performance. "Rick was excited about how [Richards] played and how he responded to the pressure of playing that type of game with the Tampa Bay general manager watching and evaluating him. It was a test and I think Rick enjoyed the outcome." Having seen Richards "pass this test," as Ludzik put it, gave

Dudley the confidence and the fortitude to press the Lightning organization and convince upper management that Richards was worth signing at a first-year salary in the range of $900,000.

In the end, both sides came together at the eleventh hour. Richards signed a three-year contract averaging just under a million dollars a year. The Lightning had secured the services of another potential franchise player. It was the beginning of another new chapter in Brad Richards's hockey odyssey—an odyssey that started in Wilcox, Saskatchewan, and now, with Brad just past his twentieth birthday, was taking him to sunny Florida.

REGULAR SEASON STATISTICS (RIMOUSKI OCÉANIC)

YEAR	GP	G	A	Pts
1997-98	68	33	82	115
1998-99	59	39	92	131
1999-00	63	71	115	186

PLAYOFF STATISTICS (RIMOUSKI OCÉANIC)

YEAR	GP	G	A	Pts
1997-98	19	8	24	32
1998-99	11	9	12	21
1999-00	13	13	24	37

OFF TO TAMPA BAY

AFTER A MEMORIAL CUP CELEBRATION BACK IN RIMOUSKI, FOLLOWED BY A PERIOD OF SUMMER REST ON PRINCE EDWARD ISLAND, RICHARDS TRAVELLED TO FLORIDA TO BE REUNITED WITH LECAVALIER AND BEGIN THE NEXT STAGE OF HIS CAREER. THE BEGINNING OF LIGHTNING TRAINING CAMP WAS MORE THAN HIS INDOCTRI-NATION INTO THE NHL; IT ALSO MEANT THE REALIZATION OF A GOAL HE AND HIS FRIEND HAD SHARED SINCE THEY WERE FOURTEEN YEARS OLD, PLAYING BANTAM HOCKEY BACK IN WILCOX. RICHARDS AND LECAVALIER HAD, IN MANY WAYS, GROWN UP TOGETHER PLAYING HOCKEY, AND FROM THE TIME THEY FIRST MET THEY BOTH DREAMED OF PLAYING TOGETHER IN THE NATIONAL HOCKEY LEAGUE. FINALLY, IT WAS ABOUT TO HAPPEN.

But in the two years apart the young players had changed. Richards came to camp full of confidence after his storybook final season with the Océanic. Lecavalier, however, was already feeling the negative effects of bearing so much pressure at such an early age. During that first training camp, Richards and Lecavalier worked closely with coach Steve Ludzik on aspects of the game, searching for ways to fine-tune both their offensive play and their defensive play without the puck. "Every morning in

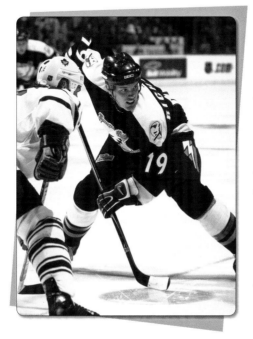

camp, we had the coffee club," said Ludzik. "I would ask Brad and Vinny to come to my office early with their coffee and we would go over their defensive responsibilities, their down-low coverage," said Ludzik. "I didn't want to take away from what Brad brought to the table offensively and fortu-nately it didn't. From the outset he played strong defensive hockey. Better than many of us expected...that rarely happens for twenty-year-old rookies."

When the season began, Richards was quick to adjust to his new league and team. Playing in just his second NHL game, Richards scored his first career goal on October 8, 2000, against Vancouver as the Lightning lost 5–4 to the Canucks. "We were there for his first goal and his first game," said Glen as he recalled seeing his son wear the Lightning jersey for the first time. "He gave us the stick and the puck from the goal against Vancouver and that was just a special moment for our family."

Soon, Richards was averaging twenty minutes of ice time each game, on his way to a sixty-two-point rookie season. Lecavalier, playing all but fourteen games, would finish the season with fifty-one points, which gave him an average of forty-eight points per season over what was now a three-year career. Ludzik says within weeks of the season starting he could see the differences in the two players, differences that were mostly related to confidence and the disproportionate amount of pressure on Lecavalier to become an instant superstar. "When Lecavalier first came to Tampa Bay the owner at the time said Vinny was going to be the Michael Jordan of hockey. It put unbelievable pressure on him and over time, when he didn't live up to the billing, he began to lose his confidence. Richards was different. He was coming off an unbelievably successful junior season. He was on a bad team so that meant he got optimal playing time, and slowly, because of his work ethic and these other factors, he was positioned to have a successful rookie season."

The NHL's Rookie of the Month for October, Richards's sixty-two points—twenty-one goals and forty-one assists—led the NHL in rookie scoring. The only Lightning player to appear in all eighty-two games, he set new franchise rookie records for goals, assists, and points, and at twenty years old, he was the second-youngest player in NHL history to lead his team in scoring. Richards also had a seven-game scoring streak from January 29 to February 13, 2001, totalling ten points over that span. Not surprisingly, he was a finalist for the 2001 Calder Trophy as the league's top rookie. However, that June the award went to San Jose Sharks goaltender Evgeni Nabokov, who finished his first NHL season with thirty-two wins, six shutouts, and 2.19 goals against average. While Richards finished second, he had served notice to his team and the rest of the league that he was a young star in the making and a player to be reckoned with in the years to come.

For Rick Dudley, it was the best and worst of times. The Lightning finished the season with just fifty-nine points and out of the playoffs for the fifth straight season, and Dudley fired head coach Steve Ludzik. But Dudley knew that with Richards and a young stable of rising, talented players, better times for the Tampa Bay Lightning were not that far away. He was also thankful that he and his organization had not made a fateful error the previous June by allowing their future franchise player to go unsigned. "I remember during Brad's rookie year, about twenty games into the season, Steve Ludzik and [assistant coach] John Torchetti were sitting in my office going over our roster. We all agreed

PREVIOUS PAGE: Adjusting to the NHL wasn't too difficult for the twenty-year-old Richards: he scored his first NHL goal in his second game.

that Brad was our best player, the best two-way player, the best player, period. We knew then that he was going to be special."

Richards was also fast proving himself to be an intense competitor and a natural leader. Calling Richards "an incredibly proud athlete," Dudley says it became evident very early in Richards's NHL career, like it had when he was in junior, that he possessed a natural ability to take his game to a higher level at crucial times. Already, even in his rookie year, on a young team trying to learn how to win, Richards was, in Dudley's opinion, a player who could always be counted on, especially in critical situations. "That's the best thing about Brad Richards," said Dudley. "When his team needs him that's when he's at his best. He's so smart, so cerebral. That first year the coaching staff and

his teammates always wanted him on the ice in crucial situations."

Ludzik, who was gone before Richards's sophomore season, put it this way: "He really is a rare superstar... what you see is what you get. His demeanor is very even and calm and every night you know what you are going to get. When I wrote the name Brad Richards on the Lightning lineup card I knew exactly what to expect from Brad. He's what every young player should aspire to be."

Following his successful rookie season Richards, along with Lecavalier, travelled to Europe once again, this time to play for Team Canada at the 2001 IIHF World Hockey Championship in Germany. Although Canada finished a

2000-01 Regular Season Statistics	
Games	82
Goals	21
Assists	41
Points	62

Back-to-back sixty-two-point seasons in his first two years in the NHL cemented Richards's potential as a star player.

disappointing fifth at the tournament, Richards finished tied with Scott Walker for the lead in team scoring with six points (three goals, three assists).

The 2001–02 season, Richards's second, brought with it a new head coach in Tampa Bay. A Calder Cup champion with the American Hockey League's Rochester Americans in 1996, John Tortorella had also spent nine of the previous eleven seasons as an NHL assistant coach, with stops in Buffalo, Phoenix, and New York. With the firing of Ludzik, Tortorella was finally given his first opportunity as an NHL head coach, inheriting the league's youngest team, a squad many considered full of potential but still several years away from being a serious Stanley Cup contender.

A no-nonsense personality never afraid to speak his mind to both his players and the media, Tortorella made headlines from the start. He placed heavy demands on his young team that first season—challenging them to improve and take the next step in their hockey development. Acknowledging there were "bumps" in his approach with players like Lecavalier and to a lesser extent Richards, Tortorella's coaching style brought results that first year. Although the Lightning missed the playoffs for the sixth straight season, they did improve by ten points.

Once again Richards led the team on offence, matching his rookie production. Traditionally a slow starter throughout his hockey career, Richards scored twice in the Lightning's first two games on his way to another sixty-two-point season. In his sophomore season and still

just twenty-one years old, Richards also led his team with 82 games played, 42 assists, and 251 shots on goal. In addition to his offensive production, Richards improved his game in another crucial area—durability. In a league where many players wear down because of fatigue, he finished the year tied for ninth in post-Olympic-break scoring, totaling twenty-six points in his final twenty-four games. There were other notable achievements that season: Richards posted twelve multi-point games and also logged a ten-game point-scoring streak from February 26 to March 18. Also, perhaps as important as his consistent production over a two-year span was Richards's dramatic increase in game-by-game ice time. During his rookie year Ludzik started putting Richards on the ice for twenty minutes each game. In 2001–02, Tortorella continued the trend, as Richards finished the season by leading Lightning forwards with an average of 19:47 per game, fifth highest in the NHL among forwards. He also played more than twenty minutes in thirty-six games, including a career high 27:15 in Tampa Bay's 2–0 loss at Chicago on January 4. With the season over, and still two months shy of his twenty-second birthday, Richards had proven himself to be one of the game's brightest young prospects. Tortorella says the sophomore forward showed him skills comparable to one of the NHL's top players. "From the first time I saw him I always compared him to Peter Forsberg in the way he sees the ice, the way he can see the goal at times," said Tortorella. "His play away from the puck and his physical aspects are where I wanted him to improve, and like Forsberg did early in his career, he keeps finding ways to protect the puck better."

Former Flyers head coach Craig Ramsay was Tortorella's assistant coach from 2001 to 2007 and saw Richards assume an on-ice leadership role as his second season progressed, mostly as a result of his strong play on special teams. "At the time he was still a young player, but he always stepped beyond himself. I think John [Tortorella] did a great job getting him on the power play and penalty kill," recalled Ramsay. "What makes him special now and what set him apart during those early years was that when Brad goes on the power play and penalty kill he believes he is going to make a good play.

Now, he's deep in his career and when you watch him block shots shorthanded or perform so well with the man-advantage, it's all part of an evolution that started during those early years. It's not an easy job. It takes courage and it was special to see. We all noticed, and it served him well when it came to establishing his confidence as a player and in earning the confidence of his teammates. It was great to see."

Instead of comparing Richards to Forsberg, Ramsay looked further back in NHL history, comparing him to a former Buffalo Sabres teammate

It didn't take Brad Richards long to attract the attention of those around the NHL. John Tortorella says Richards immediately reminded him of Peter Forsberg.

2001-02
Regular Season Statistics

Games	82
Goals	20
Assists	42
Points	62

from his playing days—a teammate who was instrumental in bringing the Murray Harbour native into the NHL in the first place. "After spending some time with him, he reminded me of Rick Dudley," said Ramsay. "They are pretty much the same size, have the same presence and, like Brad, when Rick played, he was a seventy- to ninety-point-a-year player...and they both are smart hockey players."

In addition to showcasing and honing his on-ice capabilities, Richards had also begun to establish himself as a team leader and offensive force. The only element that had eluded him so far was a chance to perform in the post-season. That opportunity would come in his third year when the Lightning came of age and emerged as an NHL powerhouse. While there were many more exploits and heroics to come over the next two seasons, 2001–02 was the year Richards started to see his team mold itself into a winner.

"We were very young when I got here and there was no stability in the team or organization," said Richards. "It was not something I was used to, coming from Rimouski. The building was not full and there was a lot of change in the organization. But after the 2002 Olympic break we really started to play well and that led right into the start of the 2002–03 season. So I think during those last twenty-five games [in 2001–02] our young guys started to learn how to win."

After missing the playoffs in 2001, Tampa Bay general manager Rick Dudley had used the off-season to improve his team's roster. Adding some depth and experience to bolster a talented but young team were moves that would complement his inexperienced squad and would, over time, be viewed as the final pieces needed for developing a winning team. On June 10, 2001, the Lightning acquired center Vaclav Prospal from the Florida Panthers for Ryan Johnson and a sixth-round draft pick. A former thirty-two-goal scorer in the AHL, Prospal had not yet established himself as a front-line NHL forward. Over five seasons with four different teams he had averaged only twenty-seven points. In his first year with the Lightning in 2001–02, Prospal played in eighty-one games while finishing second to Richards in team scoring with fifty-five points.

One month after the Prospal trade, Dudley had also signed veteran winger Dave Andreychuk. A first-round draft pick by the Buffalo Sabres in 1982, Andreychuk had played for five different teams during a nineteen-year career, scoring 572 goals over that span. While his offensive production had diminished over his career, he did contribute. Twelve and thirteen years older than many of his new teammates, Andreychuk wasn't brought in to be an offensive threat—he came to Tampa Bay to add leadership and stability. In his first season with the Lightning, Andreychuk finished third on the team in points with thirty-eight, and third in goals with twenty-one.

Two other key components in Tampa Bay's late-season success in 2001–02 were goaltender

Nikolai Khabibulin and defenseman Dan Boyle. Acquired in a trade with the Phoenix Coyotes on January 14, 2000, Khabibulin would play in just two games for the Lightning through the remainder of that season. But in 2001–02, Tortorella made him Tampa Bay's number-one goalie. He responded by playing in seventy games, winning twenty-four, while posting a 2.36 goals against average. Boyle came to the team in January 2002, and quickly became Tampa Bay's best and steadiest defenseman.

With Khabibulin, Andreychuk, Boyle, and Prospal on the team, Dudley was slowly putting together a team that was positioned to make a move in the NHL standings. Suddenly, a troubled franchise that had gone six years without making the playoffs featured a mix of youth and talent with a blend of proven NHL veterans. Dudley's game plan was transparent: adhere to the overall philosophy of placing an emphasis on speed and skill, but enhance those team attributes by adding depth and character.

Richards and the Lightning began the 2002–03 season with some new personnel and a new confidence. They went 7–1–2 in their first ten games.

However, Dudley would not be around to see his revamped team attempt to reach the post-season. In February of 2002 he resigned, resurfacing three months later in Miami as the general manager of the Florida Panthers. Dudley would remain in close contact with Richards. "I still call him to ask about players," said Dudley, now an assistant general manager with the Chicago Blackhawks. "One example is Juraj Kolnik. They played together in Rimouski, Brad knew him well, and we [the Panthers] were looking at him for 2002. I talked to Brad, asked his advice, and then signed Juraj. As of 2006 he's still with Florida and that partly goes back to Brad's recommendation. He's pretty sharp." Dudley was now gone, but he left the team positioned to succeed. Richards, Lecavalier, Andreychuk, and Khabibulin were poised to lift the Lightning back into the Stanley Cup playoffs.

A strong start to the season can carry a team far. It can set the stage for a successful drive toward the playoffs, help build confidence and momentum, and create a buffer for any prolonged slumps. In 2002, the Lightning, looking for solid start to the season, got one. On October 10 they opened on the road with a 4–3 overtime victory over Dudley's Florida Panthers. Richards put the Lightning on the scoreboard early, scoring the team's first goal of the season at the 6:08 mark of the first period. Twenty days later, Tampa Bay had a 7–1–2 record and Richards had scored one goal while adding five assists.

The team was coming of age; the talent stockpiled by high draft selections was finally providing successful results. By complementing the young team with trades and free agent signings, the Lightning also had solid leadership, beginning with Andreychuk. The former fifty-goal scorer took on the role of a third-line checking forward and led the team on the ice, on the road, and behind closed doors. Named captain before the 2002–03 season, the veteran set new locker-room rules and guidelines for the young team to follow. The first and most important rule was respecting the Lightning logo in the middle of the locker-room floor. Players were forbidden from walking on the insignia and instead had to walk around it. Failure to respect this rule resulted in player fines being levied by the captain himself, and even the media and visiting personnel were forced to adhere to this new regulation. It was also no longer permitted to have game sheets delivered to the locker room between periods or after games. In Andreychuk's view, those concerned with individual statistics were not team players.

Richards, now in his third NHL season, continued to prove himself physically durable and equipped to handle the eighty-two-game

grind that comes with being an NHL player. When the season started in Miami, Richards played in his 165th consecutive NHL game. That streak would not be snapped until January 17, 2003, at 208 consecutive games played, the second longest in franchise history behind Rob Zamuner's 226 straight games. It was just one of several career highlights established by Richards during the regular season. Six points in his first ten games sent him on his way to a career high seventy-four points, third best on the team. By surpassing the sixty-point plateau, he became the only player in Lightning history to score sixty points in three straight seasons. Richards also proved his ability to anchor the power play, finishing the season tied for first in the NHL in power play assists with thirty-four and sixth in power play points with thirty-eight. And just like in his rookie and sophomore seasons, Richards continued to log a lot of ice time, seeing more than twenty minutes in thirty-eight games, playing a season high 25:16 at Detroit on March 3. Also, for the second time in his career, and second straight season, he recorded a ten-game scoring streak.

In the end, Andreychuk, Richards, and the Lightning would turn a significant corner in the short history of the Tampa Bay franchise. The team would finish the 2002–03 season with thirty-seven wins and ninety-five points, in first place in the Southeast Division and third overall in the NHL's Eastern Conference. In the Stanley Cup playoffs for the second time in franchise history, and for the first time in seven seasons, the Lightning drew the Washington Capitals as their first-round opponent.

On April 10, 2003, Tampa Bay and Washington opened their best-of-seven first-round series at the St. Pete Times Forum and the Capitals skated to an easy victory. The Lightning fired twenty-eight shots at Capitals goaltender Olaf Kolzig and Kolzig stopped all of them as his team won 3–0. Robert Lang scored twice for the Capitals, who had won three of five regular season games against the Lightning. Playing in his post-season debut, Richards logged 20:14 of ice time, third most among Tampa Bay forwards. Two nights later, in game two, the Lightning found a way to score on Kolzig on three occasions, while upping their shot total to forty-three. Richards assisted on Andreychuk's third period goal and increased his ice time to 21:35. However, it was not enough as Jaromir Jagr scored twice and added four assists, leading Washington to a 6–3 win and a 2–0 series lead with the series shifting to the MCI Center in Washington, D. C.

On the road, and faced with a must-win situation against the Capitals, the Lightning blew three one-goal leads before hanging on for a 4–3 overtime win in game three to pull to within striking distance in the series. Richards was held pointless but pal Vincent Lecavalier carried the day, scoring the game winner at the 2:29 mark of the first overtime period to lift his team to its third post-season victory in its eleven-year existence. Lecavalier's goal was a dramatic turning point and an eventual series saver. Losing in overtime and being down 3–0 in the series would have been devastating and most likely an insurmountable challenge for such a young team. Conversely,

the dramatic victory proved a turning point in the series. Tampa Bay won games four and five by respective scores of 3–1 and 2–1. In game six on April 20, the Lightning trailed 1–0 with less than five minutes to go in the third period, when Richards assisted on Andreychuk's game-tying power play goal at the 15:54 mark. What came next was almost fifty minutes of scoreless hockey. The deadlock was finally broken at 4:03 of triple overtime when Martin St. Louis scored Tampa Bay's fourth power play goal of the series, lifting the team to the second round of the playoffs and helping to erase the pain of the franchise's years of futility. "It's a huge thing for the organization, but I'm concerned with those twenty-six guys right now," John Tortorella said following the game six victory. "It's a great stepping stone for those guys, the core people, the young people who have only been around three or four years."

The young Lightning team now faced a daunting challenge in the form of the New Jersey Devils. Heavily favoured heading into the second round, the eventual Stanley Cup-champion Devils would dispatch the Lightning in five games, but there were signs for optimism for Tampa Bay. First, the series was actually much closer than the four-games-to-one outcome would indicate, as two of Tampa Bay's defeats came in overtime (the fifth game, won by the Devils, went to triple overtime). After game five, Tortorella again put his young team's advancements in perspective. "We've made tremendous steps," Tortorella said. "This is how you build. These are the steps you need to take to become an organization like we played against tonight and through this series,

2002-03

Regular Season Statistics

Games	82
Goals	17
Assists	57
Points	74

Playoff Statistics

Games	11
Goals	0
Assists	5
Points	5

one of the model organizations in the league. These are the steps you need to go through." It was also a necessary first step for Richards, and like many of his teammates he rose to the occasion and enjoyed a productive playoff run. In the series loss to New Jersey, Richards increased his production to three points in the second round, up from two points in the six-game series with Washington.

TSN's play-by-play announcer Gord Miller called several Lightning games during the 2002–03 Stanley Cup playoffs and came away convinced this was a young team on the rise, perhaps only a year away from being a serious championship contender. "I watched the Capitals series and the way they battled was impressive," said Miller. "Then I did some of the games against the Devils. Keep in mind this was the eventual Stanley Cup champion [the Lightning] were playing. I could tell, and so could many others, that this was a good team. It was a team to keep your eye on for the next season."

It was becoming increasingly apparent that the Tampa Bay hockey market was also enjoying the performance of the young team. When Richards broke into the league in 2000–01, the Lightning attendance averaged 14,907, an improvement of 1,300 fans per game from the previous season. Then, in his second and third seasons, the attendance improved again to an average of 15,366 and 16,545, respectively. After a decade of watching inept teams, the fans in the Tampa Bay area finally appeared ready to embrace their team.

The 2002–03 season was over. The Lightning had won a combined forty-two games in the regular and post-seasons and had proven that it was a young and highly skilled team on the cusp of breaking through as a powerhouse in the league, an upstart squad that many hockey insiders now predicted could compete for a championship the following season. After three solid and steadily improving seasons, Richards had established himself as a team leader, offensive force, and key ingredient for the exciting Lightning. The 2003–04 season would see the Stanley Cup hoisted by a Florida-based team for the first time in NHL history. It would also be a year in which Brad Richards elevated his play to a level that placed him alongside the best players in the game.

ROAD TO THE STANLEY CUP

IF THEY HAD SERIOUS DESIGNS ON TAKING THEIR REGULAR SEASON PLAY TO ANOTHER LEVEL, THE LIGHTNING WERE IN NEED OF ANOTHER FAST START IN 2003. THEY, AND ESPECIALLY RICHARDS, GOT ONE—IN ALL ASPECTS OF THEIR GAME.

Tampa Bay's 2003–04 season opened at home on October 10 against the Boston Bruins, a game the Lightning won 5–1 on the strength of Richards's three points (one goal, two assists) and Nikolai Khabibulin's twenty-nine saves. By the time Tampa Bay had played its eleventh game of the season on November 8 against Pittsburgh, the Lightning had eight wins, two losses, and one tie. Richards, who had battled the "slow starter" label throughout his professional and junior career, was off to the best start of his NHL career, with ten points (two goals, eight assists) and a plus-three rating.

As successfully as the season began, though, there would soon be troubling signs—a prolonged slump doused with locker-room controversy. It would prove to be a mid-season test for a young and seemingly fragile hockey team. On November 23 the Lightning travelled to Carolina, riding a three-game winning streak and sporting an 11–3–2 record. That night, the Hurricanes outshot the Lightning 37–21 while the teams skated to a scoreless overtime tie. Two nights later, Tampa Bay was once again held scoreless, losing 2–0 at home to the New York Rangers. Being held scoreless over a two-

The plus-minus rating

When an even-strength or shorthanded goal is scored, every player on the ice for the team scoring the goal is credited with a plus one. Every player on the ice for the team scored against gets a minus one. A player's overall total is calculated by subtracting the minuses from the pluses. A high plus total suggests a player is good defensively.

game stretch would be the start of an abysmal six-week slump that saw the team win just four out of twenty games, dropping their record to 15–15–6 while being outscored as a team 48–30. In addition, the relationship between Lecavalier and coach John Tortorella was becoming strained.

On December 20, the Lightning lost 2–1 to the Dallas Stars, the team's fifth defeat in six games, dropping their record to 3–9–2 since the scoreless tie against the Hurricanes. Three nights later, with his team trailing Boston 1–0 in the second period, Tortorella decided it was time to send a message and make an example out of one of his players. That player turned out to be Vincent Lecavalier. After totalling fourteen points with a plus-three rating through his first seventeen games, Lecavalier, like his teammates, had slumped, scoring just four points over his next twelve games while dropping to a minus-one. Five minutes into the second period, Tortorella told his twenty-four-year-old centre to take a seat on the bench, and left him there for most of the remainder of the game. After the game, the third-year head coach explained his decision: "He has to start learning again to play with intensity and within the team concept, plain and simple. If he doesn't, he sits."

Lecavalier continued to sit. Three nights later, during a Boxing Day loss to the Atlanta Thrashers, he played just fourteen minutes. Then, on January 3, 2004, during a 6–1 Tampa Bay victory over Philadelphia, Lecavalier played

less than thirteen minutes, almost six minutes below his average ice time from the previous season. But the victory over the Flyers proved a turning point in the season. The team would go on to win six of its next seven games and then nine straight games between February 23 and March 6, on its way to finishing the year in first place in the NHL's Southeast Division with a 46–22–8 record, good enough for an Eastern Conference–best 106 points.

Like his teammates, Richards had also endured a lengthy slump in December, scoring just two goals while adding five assists over the twenty-game span. His slump ended in the 6–1 win over Philadelphia, with Richards leading all scorers with three assists in the game (the fifth time in his career he has recorded three assists in one game).

Lecavalier, too, was part of the turnaround, transforming his play and responding to the benching. Over his final fifty-two games, he totaled forty-eight points. More importantly, he also heeded his coach's demand to play with more intensity, while improving his plus-minus rating from minus three to plus twenty-four.

Another turning point came by way of coincidence. TSN's Gord Miller points to a little-known, behind-the-scenes drama that involved Khabibulin and backup goaltender John Grahame, who had seen an increase in playing time resulting from Khabibulin's poor play. "When the team was struggling they were also struggling with their goaltending," said Miller. "It got to the point where John Grahame was about to be the number-one guy, or least

he was starting to get a lot more time. Then on a road trip Grahame missed a team flight, and Khabibulin got the next start. After that [Khabibulin] started playing well and that was a big part of the turnaround."

In a season in which the Lightning had set a new mark for most points in franchise history, Richards set another new career best, finishing third in team scoring with twenty-six goals and fifty-three assists for seventy-nine points, cracking the NHL's top ten in scoring. He also set career highs in plus-minus at plus-eleven, short-handed goals with one, game-winning goals

with two, and average ice time with 20:25 per game (second among NHL forwards). Richards also finished tied for second on the team with six game-winning goals and first in shots with 244 while playing in all eighty-two games for the third time in his career (and eighty games or more for the fourth straight season). He also showcased an ability to get hot with seven three-point games and a seven-game assist streak from February 17 to February 28 (nine assists), the second longest in team history.

With the regular season over, the Lightning headed to the Stanley Cup playoffs as one of

Richards and the rest of the Lightning entered the 2003–04 playoffs as one of the hottest teams in the league.

TAMPA BAY LIGHTNING ATTENDANCE

As the Lightning's fortunes rose, so too did their average attendance, especially after the arrivals of Brad Richards, Vincent Lecavalier, and Martin St. Louis. In their inaugural season Tampa Bay played at the eleven-thousand seat Expo Hall. Over the next three years, they played their games at the Thunderdome, before moving to the twenty-thousand seat St. Pete Times Forum in 1996.

YEAR:	Record	Average attendance
1998-99	19-54-9	11,511
1999-00	19-47-9-7	13,600
2000-01	24-47-6-5	14,907
2001-02	27-40-11-4	15,366
2002-03	36-25-16-5	16,545
2003-04	46-22-8-6	17,820
2005-06	43-33-6	20,509

the hottest teams in the NHL. Their goaltender, Nikolai Khabibulin, had won twenty-eight games, recorded three shutouts, and compiled a 2.31 goals against average and a 0.915 save percentage, salvaging what had been mediocre numbers at the mid-season point.

The team's young, skilled players had all enjoyed breakthrough seasons. In addition to Richards and Lecavalier, Martin St. Louis was on his way to an NHL MVP award after scoring thirty-eight goals and adding fifty-six assists to lead the league in scoring with ninety-four points—seven points ahead of Atlanta Thrashers forward Ilya Kovalchuk. Even team captain Dave Andreychuk had his best offensive season in six years by reaching the forty-point plateau for the first time since 1997–98, providing his team with crucial secondary scoring.

As a team, the Lightning's goaltender was proving dominant, their offensive players were producing, locker-room leadership was firmly in place, and the head coach had laid down the gauntlet by challenging one of his top players at a time when it appeared the season could be hanging in the balance. Everything pointed toward an opportunity for further success in the postseason.

Round One: Tampa Bay vs. New York

In the opening round against the New York Islanders, the Lightning, having finished fifteen points ahead of their opponents, were expected to win the series in convincing fashion. They did, on the strength of their young forwards providing the offence and Khabibulin keeping the puck out of the net.

In the opening game on April 8, 2004, at the St. Pete Times Forum, the Islanders outshot the Lightning 30–18, but the Lightning's Russian netminder kicked aside everything he faced as Tampa Bay won 3–0. While being held off the scoresheet in the first game, Richards did log 22:04 in ice time (second only to teammate Cory Stillman, who was on the ice for 22:16) while finishing the game with a plus one rating.

Two nights later, New York turned the tables with a 3–0 victory on the strength on twenty-two-year-old Rick DiPietro's twenty-two saves. DiPietro earned his first playoff win and Jason

Blake scored his first two career post-season goals. Perhaps surprising to some, the series was now tied heading to Uniondale, New York, for games three and four.

In New York, Khabibulin and the Lightning defence took over, recording back-to-back shutouts to take a commanding 3–1 series lead. In game three on April 12, Richards scored the game's first goal (and his first career playoff goal) and the eventual game winner on the power play at the 3:34 mark of the first period. Richards would assist on all three Lightning goals while teammate Khabibulin stopped all twenty-four shots he faced in a 3–0 victory. Two nights later, it was more of the same as Khabibulin stopped twenty shots and Richards recorded one assist in

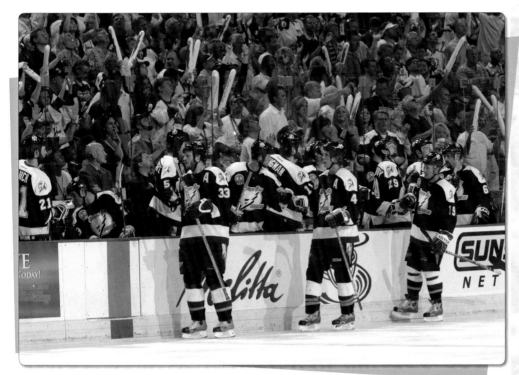

Attendance for Tampa Bay Lightning home games has increased steadily since the franchise came into the league. The fans shown here are enjoying game seven of the 2004 Stanley Cup finals.

BRAD RICHARDS – A HOCKEY STORY

another 3–0 victory. The series was heading back to Tampa Bay and the home team needed just one more win to wrap up the series.

The fifth and final game would prove to be the toughest first-round game for Tampa Bay to win—and by far the most dramatic. After skating to a 2–2 tie after sixty minutes, the teams headed to overtime. The home team was one goal away from advancing to the second round for the second straight season while the Islanders were hoping to push the series to a sixth game back on home ice. The latter would not happen. Martin St. Louis scored the game-winning goal at the 4:07 mark of the extra period to win the series for his team in five games.

Before round two Richards and the Lightning had several days of rest to find out which team they would play in the second round. It ended up being the Montreal Canadiens, who in a battle of Original Six foes, shocked the second-seeded Boston Bruins by rallying from three-games-to-one down to win their opening round series 4–3 on the strength of Jose Theodore's goaltending. Theodore allowed just three goals in the final 180 minutes of the series. But Theodore would not be the main storyline in the Tampa Bay–Montreal series. The main storyline in round two would be the elevated play of Brad Richards.

Round Two:
Tampa Bay vs. Montreal

Being the top seed in the Eastern Conference and facing a Montreal team that barely squeezed into the post-season, the Lightning were heavily favoured to win the series, but there were two troubling factors. One, Montreal had just eliminated the Boston Bruins, a team that had finished just two points behind the Lightning in the NHL's Eastern Conference during the regular season. And two, the Canadiens were the most successful team in NHL history with twenty-four Stanley Cup victories. Historically Montreal had been able to win a championship even in improbable situations (like they had in 1986 and 1993). The first-round upset over the Bruins was a subtle wake-up call to the hockey world that perhaps this, too, could be the beginning of a Montreal playoff run.

On April 23 at the St. Pete Times Forum, the Canadiens and Lightning opened their best-of-seven series, and once again Nikolai Khabibulin kept the opponents off the scoresheet entirely as the Lightning won the series opener 4–0. After a scoreless first period, Ruslan Fedotenko opened the scoring at the 2:52 mark of the second period. From that point, the well-rested Lightning dominated Montreal, scoring three goals in the final twenty-five minutes. Montreal appeared tired following their gruelling seven-game series against Boston.

Richards was held pointless in the opener. He did, however, lead his team with six shots on goal and 23:05 of ice time. Two nights later, the Lightning won again, 3–1. Once again Richards led the Tampa Bay players with 21:15 of ice time and he registered his first assist of the series, setting up Frederik Modin's goal 8:33 into the first period, a goal that would prove to

on their feet with the seconds winding down, the Lightning tied the game. With their goalie pulled for an extra attacker, Lecavalier tipped the tying goal past Theodore with just seventeen seconds to go in the third period.

The Montreal crowd was quickly silenced. The momentum swing would prove to be insurmountable for the Canadiens. The game ended just sixty-five seconds into the first overtime period when Richards scored his second goal of the game, banking in a shot off Theodore from behind the net. Just when Montreal appeared to be on the verge of getting back into the series, the Lightning scored two goals seventy-two seconds apart and were one win away from reaching the third round of the playoffs for the first time in franchise history.

Richards looks back fondly on that third game. "Game three in Montreal was by far the best atmosphere we ever played in," recalled Richards. "You haven't played hockey until you've played a playoff game in Montreal. It was that good and that special. It is just pure tradition and I wish I could go back there and push pause...it was also special because my dad was there for the overtime goal and I lived in the province for three years and knew a lot of people."

be the game-winning marker. With his team up two games to nothing, Richards and the Lightning were now heading to Montreal to one of the most hostile environments for any visiting team—the Bell Centre. It was here, back home on Canadian soil, where Richards would play two of the best back-to-back games of his career and lift his team to the Eastern Conference final.

Not surprisingly, Montreal proved to be a much tougher opponent when playing on home ice. After the teams traded first period goals in game three, Richards scored his first of the series on the power play 12:24 into the second period, giving Tampa Bay a 2–1 lead after forty minutes. Just one period away from Tampa Bay taking a 3–0 stranglehold on the series, Montreal rallied, scoring two straight third period goals to jump ahead 3–2 with just 3:37 to play in regulation. Then, while twenty-two thousand fans were

Richards's tremendous play against Montreal in the 2004 playoffs cemented his reputation as a clutch performer.

In the fourth game of the series, Montreal needed a win to avoid elimination, and even then they faced the prospect of travelling back to the St. Pete Times Forum down 3–1 in the series. For a while it appeared Montreal would in fact avoid the series sweep. Niklas Sundstrom's goal 5:46 into the first period gave Montreal a 1–0 lead. It was a lead that would hold up until the 11:57 mark of the second, when Tampa Bay's Dan Boyle scored with the man advantage to tie the game at one. Six minutes later Richards scored his third goal in two games to put his team up for good. An empty-net goal for insurance by Modin (his fifth of the post-season) with fifty-six seconds left in the third period put the game out of reach and the Lightning held on to win the fourth game 3–1, sweeping Montreal.

Richards was playing arguably the best hockey of his career. Three goals in two games, back-to-back game-winning goals, and a team-best twenty-three minutes of average ice time had lifted he and his team to the semifinal series of the Stanley Cup playoffs. After the 3–1 victory in game four, Richards, while being interviewed on *Hockey Night in Canada*, talked about the previous thrill of winning a Memorial Cup with Rimouski and compared it to the post-season run his team was enjoying in 2004. "I never want to take away the memories of my teammates and friends that I made in junior, so that will always be special. But this is the NHL. There is so much tradition here, and to finally be in the Eastern Conference final, it's going to be so exciting."

Richards also was quick to point out his team had only advanced one round further than the previous year and was still facing a tough challenge if it hoped to win the 2004 Stanley Cup. "I don't think we're content," said Richards. "I think we were last year after the first round. I think that's what happened to us against New Jersey [in 2003]."

Within minutes of the series ending, coach John Tortorella was already looking toward his next unknown opponent and basking in what appeared to be a strategic advantage over the winner of the Philadelphia–Toronto series, a series that would last six games, meaning a few extra days of rest for his team. "To get a series done in four straight in the second round is certainly going to help us because we have some guys banged up." Philadelphia would eventually dispatch Toronto, setting up a Flyers–Lightning Eastern Conference final. The winner would advance to the Stanley Cup final.

Round Three:
Tampa Bay vs. Philadelphia

Having a healthy and rested team is of paramount importance during the playoffs. The Lightning's nine-day break before the conference final was well timed and afforded the squad a rare opportunity to prepare for the most important seven games in the short history of the franchise. If there was a concern for Richards, it may have been the actual timing of the layoff. He was healthy and on a roll and didn't seem to need the break. He was also his team's hottest scorer in the final two games against Montreal and now the question was: Would the nine-day layoff cause a break in his playoff momentum? The answer became evident in the opening game of the 2004 Eastern Conference final at the 13:34 mark of the third period. Playing at even strength, Richards scored his fifth goal of the playoffs (and tenth point) to put his team on top 2–1, en route to a 3–1 victory. However, although his team won the opener and appeared to be sharp, Richards admitted the Lightning were a bit anxious during the opening minutes and would need to improve their play as the series progressed. "I think, overall, if you ask a lot of guys, I don't think they felt as good as they thought they might," Richards said after the game. "But at the same time, as the game went on, I think our game kind of calmed down and we played a little bit better."

Two nights later, Philadelphia's head coach Ken Hitchcock called his team's performance "a step in the right direction." The Flyers rebounded with a solid 6–2 victory holding Richards pointless for the first time since Tampa Bay's 4–0 series opening victory over Montreal on April 23. The 6–2 victory also ended the Lightning's franchise record eight-game playoff winning streak and halted Khabibulin's ten-game playoff run without allowing more than three goals. Khabibulin, who had four shutouts and a 1.00 goals against

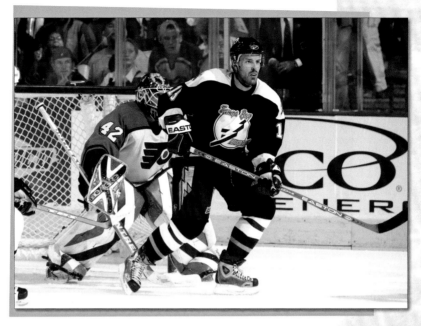

average before the game, lasted just over twenty-six minutes, allowing four goals on just twelve shots. The series was now even at one, but given that he was sporting a 1.33 goals against average and 0.950 save percentage, Khabibulin's premature exit in game two did not have any impact on the confidence of his teammates. "Habby's [Khabibulin] not going to stop them all," Tampa Bay defenceman Dan Boyle said. "We got stunned early, and we never recuperated."

The Lightning had forty-eight hours to regroup from the stunning loss. The series was now shifting to Philadelphia, an unfriendly locale for visiting teams at the best of times given the notoriously vocal nature and intensity of Flyers fans. The Tampa Bay Lightning were now facing their first dose of adversity since losing the second game of the opening round against the New York Islanders.

Brad's Lightning had a difficult time against the Philadelphia Flyers in the Eastern Conference final.

In game three the Lightning bounced back with a convincing 4–1 win to take a 2–1 series lead. Richards assisted on Cory Stillman's goal 12:56 into the first period and then scored his sixth goal of the postseason 8:20 into the third period. Most crucial for Tampa Bay in the victory was the performance of Khabibulin. Two nights after being pulled early in the second period, the Lightning netminder stopped twenty-four of twenty-five shots directed at him to improve his 2004 playoff record to 10–2.

Two days later, Khabibulin was solid again, stopping twenty-three of twenty-six shots, but the Flyers held on for a gutsy 3–2 home ice win. Richards was held scoreless in the game and now the series was shifting back to Tampa Bay tied 2–2.

In game five of the see-saw tilt, the pendulum swung back in Tampa Bay's favour, and once again the Lightning won on the strength of Richards's red-hot scoring touch. Twenty-four seconds into the second period and then 6:48 later, Richards scored back-to-back power play goals (the second marker was the game winner) for his seventh and eighth goals of the playoffs. Tampa Bay moved to within one win of reaching the Stanley Cup Final with the 4–2 topping of Philadelphia.

But in game six back at the Wachovia Centre in Philadelphia, the Flyers rebounded with a dramatic 5–4 overtime victory to push the conference final to the maximum seventh and deciding game. In a game that featured one assist by Richards, the Lighting were leading 4–3 with less than two minutes to play in the third period when Keith Primeau tied the game at four at the 18:11 mark to force extra time. Then, with 1:12 left to play in the first overtime period, and his team needing a win to stave off elimination, Simon Gagne beat Khabibulin to end it and set up the winner-take-all deciding game on Lightning home ice.

In game seven, the Lightning outplayed the Flyers but barely escaped with a victory. Outshooting Philadelphia 32–23 over three periods, Tampa Bay led 2–0 after thirty minutes of hockey thanks to goals by Ruslan Fedotenko and Fredrik Modin (Richards assisted on both goals). But Kim Johnsson's second goal of the playoffs at 10:16 of the second period pulled the Flyers to within one goal after forty minutes, setting the stage for a gut-wrenching third and final period. In the final frame Khabibulin kicked aside the seven shots he faced and the Lightning held on for a 2–1 win to take the series 4–3.

A team that had failed to qualify for the playoffs in nine of its first ten seasons in the NHL was now in the Stanley Cup final—and Richards was leading the way. Through the first three rounds of the playoffs, he was averaging better than a point per game, with seventeen points through the Lightning's first sixteen playoff games. And the best was yet to come.

SEIZING THE MOMENT

FOR ALL OF THE TALK ABOUT THE RESURGENT TAMPA BAY LIGHTNING, THEIR OPPONENTS IN THE 2004 STANLEY CUP FINAL HAD AN EVEN MORE COMPELLING RAGS-TO-RICHES NHL COMEBACK STORY.

When the Flames moved from Atlanta to Calgary in 1980, they immediately became a model of success in the NHL, reaching the post-season fifteen out of sixteen years and winning the Stanley Cup in 1989. Beginning in 1996–97, the team fell on hard times, missing the playoffs for seven straight years while going through five head coaches during that span. In 2003–04, with Darryl Sutter at the helm as the head coach and general manager, the Flames rebounded by winning forty-two regular season games, then followed that performance by stringing together twelve wins in nineteen playoff games to earn their third trip to the league finals in eighteen years.

Richards and the Lightning didn't care who they would play in the final as much as where they would play. Calgary was a Canadian team, and that geographic dynamic was appealing for Richards and his teammates. "You could see early in the playoffs that Calgary was playing really well as a team so we were not really surprised to be playing the Flames," said Richards. "But we were happy because we got to play in Canada and after beating Montreal it was something we wanted to do again. It is great to play up there in the playoffs." Flames versus Lightning did not rise to the level of a New York versus Los Angeles marquee matchup, but it did provide a signal to other more successful teams that the NHL had now achieved a new level of parity, affording even small market teams a realistic pursuit of a championship.

In the series opener at Tampa Bay, the Flames dominated the Lightning by winning 4–1, leaving Tampa Bay trailing in a series for the first time in the 2004 playoffs. Richards recorded an assist on Tampa Bay's lone goal in the third period and after the game coach Tortorella admitted his team was "jittery at the start."

In game two, the jitters were gone and once again it was Richards leading the way by scoring the game-winning goal—his ninth goal of the playoffs—as Tampa Bay held on for a 4–1 victory to even the series at one. After the game, Richards highlighted the play of Lecavalier, who had two assists and played by far his most physical post-season game. "Throughout the game he was physical. It kind of brings everybody on the same page," Richards said. Tortorella, the man who had benched Lecavalier during the regular season for not committing himself to defensive hockey, praised his young centre for elevating his play at the most crucial time, with the Lightning looking to avoid a 2–0 series deficit before embarking on a cross-continent trip to Calgary for game three. "I thought he showed a

physical presence, and you could just see him maturing, saying to the team, 'Follow me.'"

In game three at a wild Calgary Saddledome, the Flames relied on their hot goaltender to move within two wins of the championship. Miikka Kiprusoff stopped twenty-one shots to record his fifth shutout in the 2004 playoffs as the Flames blanked the Lightning 3–0.

Game four wasn't a must-win for the Lightning, but it was close. Not wanting to go down 3–1 in the series, the Lightning came out flying in the fourth game with Richards scoring his tenth goal of the playoffs at the 2:48 mark of the first period. It would prove to be yet another game-winning goal, as Khabibulin stopped all twenty-nine shots he faced, including twelve in the third period alone. Richards's goal was his seventh game-winner of the playoffs, setting a new Stanley Cup record. "You just hope to score goals and change the momentum of the game and help your team out," Richards said. "You

don't know if they're going to be game-winners. You have no control over that when you score a goal early in the game." Once again the series was tied as both teams travelled back to the St. Pete Times Forum for a pivotal game five.

The win one, lose one, pattern of the series continued in the fifth game as the Flames inched closer to their second Stanley Cup in franchise history with a 3–2 overtime victory. In a game the Lightning never led, Richards assisted on the tying goal scored by Frederik Modin thirty-seven seconds into the third period. However, Oleg Saprykin won it for the visitors with 5:20 to play in the fourth period. The series was now shifting back to Calgary and the Flames not only had regained the momentum, but they

also had home-ice advantage for the potential clinching game.

In game six, after a scoreless first period, Calgary and Tampa Bay traded two goals apiece (both by Richards) in the second and they headed to the dressing room tied. The tie held up through sixty and then eighty minutes. Then, just thirty-three seconds into the second overtime, Martin St. Louis breathed new life into his team when he scored to win the game and set up a game seven showdown. Said Tortorella after the game: "It's been a hell of a series, and it's fitting we have a game seven." The St. Louis goal did more than keep his team alive; it also completely transferred the adversity from one team to another. The Lightning had been in overtime,

Brad Richards leads the Lightning attack up the ice in game seven of the Stanley Cup finals. Richards finished the playoffs with an NHL-best twenty-six points.

in the opposing team's arena, attempting to stave off elimination. Then, after just one goal, they had momentum and were heading back to Tampa Bay with the advantage of playing the seventh game on home ice.

After nearly two months of intense playoffs, the heart-stopping pace of the sixth game surprisingly did not take Richards out of his comfort zone. On the contrary, he said he and his teammates had an almost "businesslike" approach to the game, especially during overtime. "We were really in the moment and that game was in our heads. You always try to do that but game six we knew we had nothing to lose, we had to just come together and win a game. As we got into overtime and then the double OT we were so tired it didn't really sink in how one goal could win or lose. We just tried to fight the best we could and Marty popped one. I'll never forget that game. It might have been the hardest we played all year."

Richards's parents watched game six on television back in Murray Harbour. The family plan called for an emergency trip to Tampa if game seven became necessary. "Brad had booked tickets for the family if they beat Calgary that night," said Delite. "My job was to call the travel agent and say 'Yes or no we do or don't want tickets.' On Monday we went to the Halifax airport and hoped and prayed we didn't have any delays." Their prayers answered, the extended Richards family made it to Florida with time to spare. As for turning their backs on lobster fishing during the peak season: "We gave that up for a couple of days," recalled Glen.

"We knew we could always catch some lobster but you couldn't always catch a Stanley Cup!"

In the seventh and deciding game, both teams played a tentative opening period, with Tampa Bay scoring the only goal. Ruslan Fedotenko's eleventh goal of the playoffs came on the power play at 13:31 to give the Lightning a

Brad's mother and father celebrate on the ice with their son after Brad won the Stanley Cup and Conn Smythe Trophy.

FACING PAGE: Post-season MVP Brad Richards hoists the Stanley Cup in front of the Tampa Bay fans.

Brad shows the Stanley Cup
some Island hospitality.

1–0 lead after one period. Richards picked up an assist on the goal, his twenty-sixth and final point of the 2004 Stanley Cup playoffs. Fedotenko added his twelfth of the playoffs in the second period to put the home team up by two on their way to a 2–1 series-clinching victory. The Tampa Bay Lightning, in just its twelfth year of existence, had captured the Stanley Cup.

To say the least, there was a lot happening on the ice at the St. Pete Times Forum after the Lightning's game seven victory. The crowd was deafeningly loud and the on-ice celebration reached hysterical levels. Richards looked back on the championship win lamenting the fact that every aspect of the celebration went by far too quickly. "It was a blur," said Richards. "The one thing I could take back would be that night. I would like to enjoy it more and take more in. It was rushed and with all the people around it was just crazy... I think we were young and had no idea how to enjoy it to its fullest."

With their son celebrating alongside his teammates, Glen and Delite watched from the stands, glowing with parental pride while reflecting on the hard work and sacrifice that had paved the way for this success. "I had tears of joy," said Glen. "At a time like that, a million things go through your mind. How he started, how he went away so young, all the tournaments. I remembered all the little things."

Looking back on the championship, Tortorella talked about how the young team had come together in a way no one could have imagined and succeeded in a way, that by his own admis-

sion, went beyond realistic expectations. "We stayed together for three-and-a- half years," said Tortorella. "Yes, we had our bumps, but then we started to understand each other. When we finally came together that spring it was a special thing and all of us will always enjoy that special bond." Reflecting on Richards's playoff performance, Tortorella talked about the young man's demeanor and maturity and how these qualities carried Richards through the sixty-day, twenty-three-game grind of competing in four playoff series. "His being able to handle the highs and lows were key. That's one of his strengths and it's important. He's hard on himself but he has an ability to keep things straight. He didn't get too high and didn't get too low."

Richards also referred to the "high and lows" mentioned by his head coach. He also gave perspective to the effort and focus needed for a team to capture a Stanley Cup. "The regular season is a grind but the two months of playoffs are out of this world, physically, and even more,

Murray Harbour hosted post-Stanley Cup celebrations along with Brad and his new trophies.

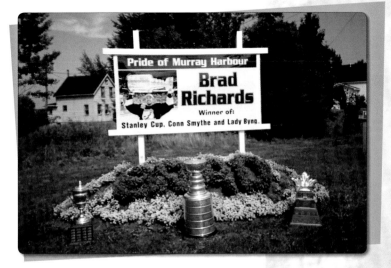

2003-04
Regular Season Statistics

Games	82
Goals	26
Assists	52
Points	78

Playoff Statistics

Games	23
Goals	12
Assists	14
Points	26

mentally," said Richards. "There are so many ups and downs, you don't sleep or eat well. You are high when you win and so low when you lose. You also live with a feeling in the pit of your stomach that you want to go away, but [once] it is over you want it back. It was two of the best months I will ever live and all I can do is hope like hell I can do it again."

Richards's twenty-six points led all scorers in the post-season and he had set a record with seven game-winning goals. He also not only set a new Lightning team record for points in a playoff season but also for most goals in the playoffs with twelve, and most power play goals in the playoffs with seven. In the moments following the initial on-ice celebration, he was named the winner of the Conn Smythe Trophy as the most valuable player in the post-season.

With the Stanley Cup celebration continuing in Tampa Bay, and only three days removed from winning game seven and being named Conn Smythe Trophy winner, Richards attended the 2004 NHL Awards at the John Bassett Theatre in Toronto. He had been nominated for the Lady Byng Memorial Trophy, awarded to the NHL player who best displays sportsmanship and gentlemanly conduct during the regular season. In 2003–04, Richards received only twelve penalty minutes in eighty-two games.

A finalist alongside teammate Martin St. Louis and Ottawa Senators captain Daniel Alfredsson, Richards won the award, his second major trophy in seventy-two hours—an accomplishment that earned the praise of longtime NHL referee Don Koharski. "Brad's got tremendous skill and talent and he minds his own business out there," said Koharski. "He doesn't take any penalties, he just plays the game. He's an ultimate team player. That's what I think the Lady Byng is about, the talented skill player who commits himself to the team and not himself. In 2003–04, that what Brad Richards was all about."

Admitting that the Lady Byng was "a trophy you don't set out to try to win," Richards says it did provide an extra thrill to what was already his most memorable hockey season. "It just happened as a bonus. Obviously it is an NHL trophy and I will never turn my nose up at that. It was a great honour to see the names on that trophy alongside mine."

A summer of Stanley Cup celebrations included a Brad Richards Day in Murray Harbour. Like many of his Lightning teammates, Richards brought the Stanley Cup to his hometown. "To see Murray Harbour go from 250 people to 15,000 was a pretty special moment for me and all my family and friends," says Richards. "PEI will always be my real home and I will always feel comfortable there. I wanted to share the Cup with my biggest supporters."

HIGH EXPECTATIONS

IN MAY OF 2004, RICHARDS, LECAVALIER, AND ST. LOUIS WERE ALL NAMED TO TEAM CANADA'S ROSTER FOR THE 2004 WORLD CUP OF HOCKEY. CANADA WON THE GOLD MEDAL WITH A WIN OVER FINLAND IN THE FINAL, MAKING UP FOR ITS LOSS TO THE AMERICANS AT THE SAME TOURNAMENT IN 1996. FOR THE SECOND TIME IN HIS CAREER, RICHARDS HAD WON A MAJOR INTERNATIONAL COMPETITION WHILE PLAYING FOR HIS COUNTRY AND ONCE AGAIN HE MADE A SIGNIFICANT OFFENSIVE CONTRIBUTION, SCORING A GOAL WHILE ADDING AN ASSIST.

Richards had won a Stanley Cup and World Cup in just three months and whether he needed a rest or not, he got one. The long-expected work stoppage in the National Hockey League became a reality in the autumn of 2004. Across North America, arenas went dark and silent. When it became apparent that neither the NHL owners nor the players were about to capitulate, and that the work stoppage would be a long-term affair, many players went overseas to play hockey. Saying "You can only golf so much," Richards decided to return to playing hockey, and signed with Ak-Bars Kazan in Russia. In time, his teammates Vincent Lecavalier and Nikolai Khabibulin also joined the Russian Elite League team, but it would be a short reunion. After registering seven points in seven games, Richards left the team and returned to Canada in December after suffering from what he called "scary pain" in his hip. Within days the injury was diagnosed as a sports hernia (weakness in the abdominal wall). Richards would require at least twelve weeks of rehabilitation, which meant his

the action in person. In the end, Rimouski failed in its bid to capture another Memorial Cup, but Richards's presence was a boost appreciated by both the players and his former coach. "He wanted to come back and see the team and watch it win," said Labonté. "He lodged at the same hotel as the team and of course came to the games. After I asked him, he also came to the dressing room to offer support. He didn't want to interfere or try to be a coach. He just wanted to show the team that he still cared for them. That meant a lot to everyone."

In the weeks following the 2005 Memorial Cup, labour harmony was finally restored in the NHL. After wiping out an entire regular and post-season, the league owners and players' association finally reached an agreement to end the lockout in June.

On October 5, 2005, a year later than originally scheduled, the Tampa Bay Lightning finally hoisted their Stanley Cup championship banner to the rafters of the St. Pete Times Forum, with more than twenty-two thousand fans on hand

2004–05 hockey season was over. "The big thing was rest and some rehab exercises and absolutely no skating," Richards said.

With a lockout and an injury putting a temporary halt to his career, Richards had plenty of time to watch hockey and luckily there was a good story-line unfolding with his old junior team—a story worth watching in person. Led by seventeen-year-old Sidney Crosby, the Rimouski Océanic were back in contention for junior hockey supremacy in 2005. After sweeping the Halifax Mooseheads in the QMJHL final, the team found itself back at the Memorial Cup for the second time in five years. Rather than watch the games on television, Richards travelled to London, Ontario, to take in

PREVIOUS PAGE: Richards and teammate St. Louis (far right) were part of Canada's tournament-winning squad in the World Cup.

ABOVE: With no end in sight to the NHL lockout, Brad signed with the Russian Elite League team, Ak-Bars Kazan, in the fall of 2004.

BELOW: Richards's Ak-Bars Kazan jersey.

watching the ceremony. In the game that followed, the Lightning continued their winning ways with a 5–2 victory over the Carolina Hurricanes. Richards wasted little time getting on the scoresheet when he scored on the power play at the 10:08 mark of the first period. The early offensive contribution was no fluke as Richards would go on to record the best performance of his NHL career, scoring twenty-three goals with sixty-eight assists for ninety-one points. His hernia injury fully healed, Richards also showcased his physical durability, playing in all eighty-two regular season games for the fourth time in five years.

As successful as 2005–06 was for Richards personally, the season proved to be a disappointment for his team as the Lightning fell to eighth place in the Eastern Conference, dropping to 92 points, from 106 points in 2003–04. There were several factors leading to the team's drop-off, but the most notable was the change in goaltenders. Nikolai Khabibulin left the team to sign as an unrestricted free agent with the Chicago Blackhawks, leaving the job to veterans Sean Burke and John Grahame, neither of whom had good years. Grahame finished the season with 3.06 goals against average with a 0.889 save percentage, while Burke, playing in thirty-five games,

While the Lightning couldn't repeat in 2005–06, Richards recorded the highest point of total of his career, scoring twenty-three goals and tallying sixty-eight assists.

had a 2.80 goals against average with a 0.895 save percentage. In just one season the Lightning had allowed sixty-eight more goals against and suddenly looked very beatable heading into the Stanley Cup playoffs against the Ottawa Senators.

The loss of Khabibulin was also a reflection of what life was like in the "new NHL." The league had changed the on-ice and off-ice rules following the lockout, and one of those rules was the impetus to the lockout itself—a salary cap. Before the work stoppage there was no cap and when the lockout ended many teams, Tampa Bay included, were forced to make tough roster decisions in order to keep their payroll below the league-imposed ceiling. Khabibulin, coming off a Stanley Cup championship and a stellar post-season, was deemed too expensive for the defending champions, and therefore was allowed to leave the team via the free agent market.

When Grahame, Burke, and the rest of the Lightning reached the playoffs in 2006, any buzz about another Stanley Cup quickly faded when the team lost in the opening round to Ottawa in five games. Even in defeat, Richards once again led the way for his team, scoring three goals with five assists in the five games played.

2006 Winter Olympics, Turin, Italy

In 2002 in Salt Lake City, Utah, Canada's men's Olympic hockey team ended a fifty-year gold-medal drought. In 2006, led once again by NHL players, Canada was favoured to repeat as Olympic hockey champions, and Richards, Lecavalier, and St. Louis were all named to Canada's roster. Wayne Gretzky was the executive director of Team Canada's Olympic hockey team and did not hesitate to add Richards. "Brad is a great player who works hard and is very unselfish," said Gretzky. "He was born to compete and is a good young man. He loves to play hockey and was a great fit for Team Canada."

Unfortunately, while Richards was a good fit on the team, the team was not a good fit for the Olympic hockey tournament. After winning their first two games against Italy and Germany by a combined score of 12–3, Canada stumbled against Switzerland, losing 2–0 and showing the entire hockey world that this Team Canada squad was vulnerable. Six days later, Canada lost another 2–0 game, this time to the Russians in the quarterfinal, and was eliminated from the competition without a medal. Richards finished the tournament as one of the bright spots for Team Canada. As TSN's Gord Miller put it, "In an Olympics where no one really did anything, Richards did very well." Playing in all six games, he scored two goals and added two assists to finish with four points, earning him praise from the man who ultimately decided he deserved to be on the team in the first place. "Brad played very well," said Gretzky. "Unfortunately, we didn't come home with the gold medal but Brad played hard and contributed."

Playing for Canada at the Olympics was a career highlight, but failing to win gold was one of the

HOCKEY CANADA RESUMÉ

Beginning in 1997 with Canada's under-18 team, Brad Richards has played for his country five times, winning championships at the 1997 Three Nations Cup and 2004 World Cup.

Year Event	GP	Goals	Assists	Points
1997 Three Nations Cup	3	0	0	0
2000 IIHF World Junior Championship	7	1	1	2
2001 IIHF World Championship	7	3	3	6
2004 World Cup	6	1	3	4
2006 Winter Olympics	6	2	2	4

biggest disappointments in Richards's career to date. "It was a fun buildup and the excitement to be named to play on Team Canada was great," said Richards. "But when you get there and lose it really hurts the whole experience. I can't really get my head around losing."

With five successful NHL seasons under his belt, and coming off a career best ninety-one points in the 2005–06 campaign, Richards began 2006–07 like he had several other seasons—slowly. The Lightning opened their season on the road with a 3–2 shootout win over the Atlanta Thrashers. Richards assisted on Tampa Bay's first goal of the season by Ryan Craig, but then failed to register another assist until the Lightning's fifth game of the season. While teammates Vincent Lecavalier and Martin St. Louis jumped out to quick starts and posted 108- and 102-point seasons, respectively, Richards struggled at times playing under a new multi-million-dollar contract, finishing the season with seventy points (twenty-five goals, forty-five assists). Twenty-one points below

his total from the year before, and his lowest production since his second season in the NHL, Richards was still the third-highest scorer on the team. But in just one year Richards's points-per-game average slipped from 1.1 to 0.85, and his plus-minus rating dropped from a respectable even (zero), to a minus nineteen.

One notable reason for the drop in Richards's production may have been the change in his supporting cast. Fredrik Modin, Richards's former linemate, was traded to the Columbus Blue Jackets in the off-season and St. Louis had moved up to the Lightning's top line. "The truth is we traded away a thirty-goal guy in Fredrik Modin," said Lightning GM Jay Feaster. "The line used to be Modin, Richards, and Martin St. Louis. Now not only does [Richards] not have Modin, he doesn't have St. Louis because [St. Louis] is playing with Vinny Lecavalier."

The Lightning finished with ninety-three points, one point ahead of their total from the year before, good for seventh overall in the Eastern

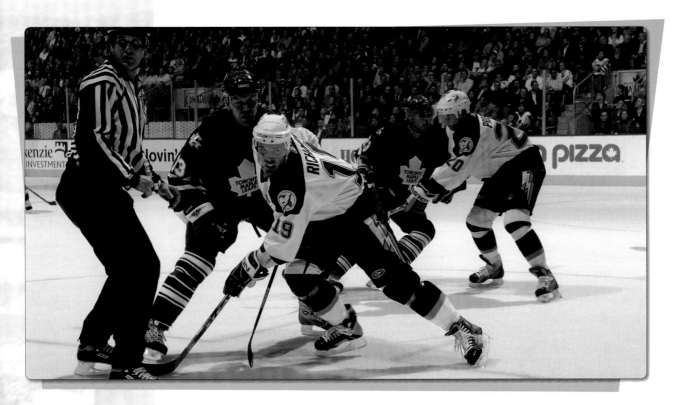

Richards found the going much tougher in 2006–07, seeing a twenty-one-point drop from his point total of a year earlier.

Conference. Tampa Bay played the second place New Jersey Devils in the opening round of the playoffs and once again, Richards elevated his post-season performance. While New Jersey would go on to win the series in six games, Richards finished with eight points (three goals, five assists), bringing his career playoff totals to forty-seven points (eighteen goals, twenty-nine assists) in forty-five career playoff games.

After the Lightning signed Richards to a new, lucrative contract in 2006, Feaster justified the contract to the Associated Press by saying that Richards had "stepped up to every challenge we have ever issued to him." The Tampa Bay Lightning were two years and two playoff disappointments removed from winning a championship, but, according to Feaster, the future was still bright in Tampa Bay because they had Brad Richards, a young player who had proven time and time again that he performed at his best in the most crucial situations.

GIVING SOMETHING BACK

RESTRICTED FREE AGENCY HAS ITS LIMITATIONS FOR NHL PLAYERS WHO HOPE TO USE THE OPPORTUNITY TO MOVE TO ANOTHER TEAM. FOR THAT TO HAPPEN A PLAYER MUST SIGN AN OFFER SHEET WITH ANOTHER ORGANIZATION, BUT THE PLAYER'S CURRENT TEAM HAS THE FIRST RIGHT TO MATCH THAT OFFER BEFORE LETTING HIM BOLT TO A NEW TEAM. SO WHEN RICHARDS WAS SCHEDULED TO BECOME A RESTRICTED FREE AGENT ON JULY 1, 2006, NOT MANY HOCKEY EXECUTIVES OR FANS EXPECTED TO SEE HIM WIND UP IN ANOTHER UNIFORM. WHAT WAS A SURPRISE WAS THE RAPIDITY WITH WHICH HIS CONTRACT SITUATION WAS RESOLVED.

On April 29 the Lightning were eliminated by the Ottawa Senators in the opening round of the Stanley Cup playoffs. The next morning, Lightning general manager Jay Feaster called Richards's agent Pat Morris to begin the process that would lead to a new five-year, $39-million deal, making him the team's highest-paid player at $7.8 million per season. "He deserves it," Tortorella told the Globe and Mail on the day the signing was announced. "There are a lot of contracts out there that I don't think players deserve. This one here, there's no question because

of what he's done and what he's able to do because there's more, and Brad knows that. I think he's going to reach down and bring that out with him to carry this organization."

Watching from afar was Rick Dudley, Feaster's ex-boss and Richards's first NHL general manager. Beyond the wealth and security, Dudley saw the signing as an acknowledgement of long-overdue respect for a player who worked hard to prove to his hockey peers that he was a bona fide NHL star and not the fringe

In January of 2007, the Hockey News (THN) published its list of 100 People of Power and Influence, and Brad Richards was number ninety-seven. In explaining the Richards selection, THN wrote: "There are a couple of prime reasons why NHL GMs watch Richards. One is his scoring touch and the other is his salary. Richards, 26, eats up more of his team's payroll than any other NHLer; his pay cheque is the benchmark that both owners and players use in salary negotiations."

PREVIOUS PAGE: A new five-year, $39-million contract signed in 2006 made Richards one of the highest-paid players in the NHL.

RIGHT: Brad with his younger cousin, Jamie Reynolds. Jamie's battle with cancer as a young child helped inspire the Richy's Rascals Suite Escape in Tampa Bay.

FACING PAGE: Richy's Rascals Suite Escape. "I absolutely love to see the kids with smiles on their faces," says Brad.

player projected by so many. "When you look at that contract he just signed, some fans may not appreciate him but Jay [Feaster] and the Tampa Bay Lighting appreciate him and that's probably all the respect Brad Richards needs. He worked hard to earn that respect, harder than a lot of people realize."

TSN's Gord Miller points to the fact that, while he sometimes gets second and third billing on the Tampa Bay team, it should be underscored that Richards, with the contract serving as proof, is now the foundation for the Tampa Bay franchise. "I have always said it, and it appears the Lightning now agree. Martin St. Louis was the MVP. Vinny Lecavalier may be the franchise player, but Brad Richards is their best player. Period."

Brad Richards could live out his life as a multi-millionaire playing hockey and driving luxury model cars and no one would criticize him for doing so. Instead, from the moment he entered the National Hockey League, Richards has worked hard to identify charitable organizations in the Tampa Bay area and in his home province of Prince Edward Island.

John Tortorella says every dollar Richards spends and every moment he devotes to sick children is a reflection of the values Tortorella believes were instilled from a very young age. "He's done so much in the community, and he's done it very quietly. I think it's all a part of how his parents brought him up and his environment from when he was young."

On the last point, Tortorella has touched the heart of the matter. Growing up in Murray

Harbour, Richards was very close with his cousin Jamie Reynolds, who was diagnosed with brain cancer at age four. Jamie died several years later. "We were neighbours and best of friends and he died way too young and I got to go on and do all these things in my life," says Richards. "That makes you wonder how everything works in this world. So when I get a chance to make kids forget their illnesses I think it is the least I can do. I absolutely love to see the kids with smiles on their faces."

Brad and his young cousin, Zachary Reynolds, with the Stanley Cup in Murray Harbour.

Delite remembers Brad, still a child, visiting Jamie at the hospital in Halifax in the days not long before he died. "The nurses would say 'You must be Brad. Jamie has been waiting for you all day.' It was very sad but very special to see these two together. Even when he was a young boy Brad always said 'If I can do something about this I will.' Now he is."

One of Richards's most visible endeavours is the Richy's Rascals Suite Escape, an outreach program for young children in the Tampa Bay area who are battling cancer. In addition to soaking up a Lightning game experience, guests at the suite are able to do arts and crafts, play video games, and they are also outfitted with Lightning clothing. Richards funds the entire Richy's Rascals project himself and has also been known to visit

his guests following games. In 2003–04, he purchased a luxury suite at the St. Pete Times Forum and immediately went to work, renovating it into what appears to be a kid's playhouse, sitting in the backdrop of a live NHL game.

"Those are the kind of things that really make you proud about your son," says his father Glen. "We would be proud anyway, but when you go down there and see him with these kids and what they've been through and then you see them in the suite with their families and having a ball, it makes you feel special that you have a son who is trying to help."

"It's the part of Brad we are most proud of," says Delite. "We were at the suite once and there were four kids and they were all pretty sick. They were just ecstatic and it was really nice to see. It's good for them and it's good for Brad to be able to do this."

Adhering to the adage "charity begins at home," Richards has also devoted his time and energy to helping people in his native province. The Brad Richards PEI Golf Classic is a summertime tournament that serves as fundraiser for the Prince Edward Island chapter of the Children's Wish Foundation as well as the Autism Society of Prince Edward Island. The Children's Wish Foundation grants the favourite wish of kids between the ages of three and eighteen who have been diagnosed with life-threatening illness. As for raising money to support the research into the cause and treatment of autism, again this is a cause that is very meaningful to the Richards family— his two cousins, Jack and Mason Mackenzie, live with autism. "The way he gives so much time to help kids tells you that money and fame hasn't changed him one bit," said friend and former teammate Thatcher Bell. "He's still Brad Richards,

Brad with his childhood idol, Joe Sakic.

a guy from Murray Harbour who hasn't forgotten where he's from."

Fast Facts

NUMBER: 19

POSITION: Centre

DATE OF BIRTH: May 2, 1980

HEIGHT: 6 feet

WEIGHT: 198 pounds

SHOOTS: left

DRAFTED: Selected by Tampa Bay, third round, sixty-fourth overall in 1998

FIRST NHL GAME: October 6, 2000, versus New York Islanders

FIRST NHL GOAL: October 10, 2000, versus Vancouver Canucks

FAVOURITE NHL ROAD CITY: Montreal

FAVOURITE NHL PLAYER: Joe Sakic

FAVOURITE NHL TEAM GROWING UP: Chicago Blackhawks

POST-JUNIOR HOCKEY CAREER HONOUR: number 19 retired by Rimouski Océanic

In their own words

Gord Miller, TSN play-by-play announcer:

"There is pride and fire. Throughout his career he has been underappreciated. He was seen as undersized, people didn't appreciate his skating and some people didn't even expect him to make the Tampa Bay team. He knows this and takes it with him whenever he plays."

John Tortorella, Tampa Bay Lightning head coach:

"Brad Richards is an incredibly proud athlete. He is grounded, respects his position in life, and understands all of the intangibles both on and off the ice."

Rick Dudley, Former Lightning general manager:

"He's one of the top forwards in the game, there's no question. He plays in Tampa Bay and not enough people get to see him. He scores five points in one game and people say 'That's nice.' He wins the Stanley Cup and the Conn Smythe award and people say, 'That's nice.' For some reason, when it comes to fan appreciation he doesn't get the respect he deserves. It's puzzling. I think he's one of the game's top players."

Shawn MacKenzie, Former Halifax Mooseheads head coach:

"Brad Richards plays such a well-rounded game. I have so much respect for the competitiveness of his game."

Steve Ludzik, Former Tampa Bay Lightning head coach:

"There are three types of players: those who watch what's happening, those who make things happen, and those who don't know what's happening. Brad Richards makes things happen."

Doris Labonté, Rimouski Océanic head coach:

"In 1999–2000...Brad had a special season. Remember this: he was the MVP of the regular season, the playoffs, and the Memorial Cup. He was also the scoring leader of the regular season, the playoffs, and the Memorial Cup. Those numbers show his teammates and coaches that he'll be there for them all the time. Not sometimes, but always."